WHAT I WISH I KNEW ABOUT LOVE

KIRSTIE TAYLOR

THOUGHT CATALOG Books

THOUGHTCATALOG.COM
NEW YORK • LOS ANGELES

THOUGHT
CATALOG
Books

Published by Thought Catalog Books, an imprint of the digital magazine Thought Catalog, which is owned and operated by The Thought & Expression Company LLC, an independent media organization based in Brooklyn, New York and Los Angeles, California.

The events, places, and conversations in this book have been recreated from memory. The chronology of events may have been compressed. When necessary, the names and identifying characteristics of individuals and places have been changed to maintain anonymity.

This book was produced by Chris Lavergne and Noelle Beams. Art direction and design by KJ Parish. Special thanks to Bianca Sparacino for creative editorial direction and Isidoros Karamitopoulos for circulation management.

Visit us on the web at thoughtcatalog.com and shopcatalog.com.

Made in the United States of America.
ISBN 978-1-949759-30-3

TABLE OF CONTENTS

FINDING A GREAT PARTNER 127

CREATING A LOVING RELATIONSHIP 181

INTRODUCTION

L ove (or pain due to a lack of love) is a theme that runs through every person's life, molding who they are and reframing the way they view the world. Yet no one teaches us about love. We're expected to know how to swim through it, when most of us can barely tread water.

I decided to write this book because I wish someone had taught me how to swim instead of having to learn the hard way: through broken hearts, late-night texts to my exes, and tear-soaked pillows. There's no book out there that gives fluff-free advice about the journey of finding a great relationship. Some books focus on the single life, others on dating, and many on relationships. But this book covers all of that. Because having written over five hundred articles on dating, relationships, and self-love, I know a thing or two about this world.

If you're like I was, feeling like a victim of my love life, rather than in control, then these words on what I've learned over the years are for you. May they teach you how to swim.

I was obsessed with the idea of love as far back as I could remember. I wanted it from my parents. From my grandmother and my aunt. I wanted it from the boy in my kindergarten class and every friend I made. But you never would've met me and thought I had this desire to be loved. I was an independent child who could entertain herself for hours as long as I was outside. I'd find tadpoles to make my pets or trees to climb. I had friends from school and in the neighborhood who I rode bikes with, but I wasn't that great at becoming close friends with any of them. My need for closeness with other people lived inside me but I didn't know how to properly express or fulfill it. But from hearing girls talk about their boyfriends as early as elementary school, I figured I could satiate my need for love through a boy. I wanted someone to call my boyfriend and care about me in the ways I saw teenagers at the mall act in their relationships.

My first taste of that kind of affection came in the fourth grade. My mom would take me to skate at the local ice rink with my friends from school and wouldn't come back to pick me up until sunset. My friends and I had free reign of the rink, along with the other kids from the surrounding schools.

On one particular day, I noticed a boy look at me while I was untying my sneakers. His cheeks became rosy as he walked over and commented that he liked my shoes. His name was Corey and he had a messy head of brunette hair. He was one grade older than me (yes, I liked older men, even in the fourth grade). He came to the rink with a group of three other boys and we combined our friend groups for the day. All of us battled it out at air hockey and challenged each other to see who could get a stuffed tiger at the claw machine (Spoiler: it was me. I've always rocked at the claw machine). Then we moved our focus over to the ice rink. A few laps into skating, Corey came up alongside me and smiled. He grabbed my hand and laced his fingers between mine. I was elated. A feeling of electricity pulsed through my body.

At the end of the night, Corey took down my number before his mom picked him up so we could stay in touch. When I got home, I waited anxiously for him to call. I imagined our future together: skating every week at the ice rink. We'd go to movies together and he'd be the boy I had my first kiss with. But days passed, then weeks. The phone didn't ring once with Corey on the other end. Each time my friends and I went to the skating rink, I'd search for him. But I never saw Corey again. You could say that was my first heartbreak.

Maybe he didn't feel the electric connection I did, or perhaps he lost the Juicy Fruit gum wrapper he'd written my number on. Either way, Corey ignited in me an intense infatuation with what I thought was love.

I didn't realize it then, but my idea of how love works was greatly shaped from that experience. I'd fallen into a romantic narrative with a boy I didn't even know the last name of. That would've been cute if I'd left that habit in elementary school, but I carried it well into my adulthood. In fact, a lot of the ways I thought love worked were wrong: from how to give it, to receiving it, to what it even looked like. Reflecting back, it really did feel like I was thrown into the deep end of a pool and faintly heard someone yell, "Good luck!" If there was ever a time to use the term "trial and error," it would be to describe my love life.

And I know I'm not alone in this.

Years of failed relationships, heartbreaks, and a lot of sadness passed before I stopped to question why love felt so painful. I didn't want to feel like a victim to love anymore, I wanted to be in control. So I took matters into my own hands.

I re-focused my energy from obsessing over trying to make people love me to learning about the subject of love. I've read thousands of articles and consumed every ounce of knowledge I could from books. If there's a case study out there about how love affects our adult lives, I've read it. With all of that new-found knowledge, I began applying it to my own life and started seeing massive changes. That's when I decided to write about my experiences. Since then, I've published over five hundred articles. I've discussed relationships and dating on podcasts and in Forbes. My work has been featured in magazines across the nation (including airports, which still blows my mind) and websites my younger self would have only dreamed of being in. It's safe to say I really do love love. So much so, I made a career from it.

Through everything I learned, I wondered why we're never taught about love: not in school, by our parents, or in the media (at least in a healthy sense). The only times I'd ever heard of people being educated on relationships was right before marriage or well into one. Essentially, two points in one's life when it's a little too late.

That's why I'm writing these words. They're for anyone finding themselves in one unhappy relationship after another, struggling with self-esteem, or needs a little help with their dating lives. This book is a culmination of everything about love I wish an older sister or quirky aunt had taught me when I was younger. So, think of me as that older sister or eccentric aunt, wine glass in hand, ready to lay it all out for you.

This book is for anyone who wants to radically change the way they experience love. I'll tear apart misguided ideas on love we learned as children. You'll be asked to answer difficult questions to gain a better understanding of why you struggle with love (including self-love). I'll talk about the best ways to go about finding a partner you deserve. After that, we'll go through how to create and maintain a healthy relationship.

I hope you benefit from the lessons I've learned and let them guide you to having fulfilling romantic relationships, friendships, and self-love anyone is capable of having. I won't lie to you and say love is easy. This book doesn't have secret answers to finding your soulmate (which I don't believe in anyway). But the words you're about to read will give you hope, understanding, and confidence to move into the world of love. This is what I wish I knew about love.

PART I

RE-WRITING THE SCRIPT ON LOVE

THE STORIES WE WERE TOLD ABOUT LOVE

As a child, I was fascinated with Julia Roberts. I'd spend hours plopped in front of my TV, watching Julia be anything from a bridesmaid to a prostitute (though I didn't know what a prostitute was at that time; I barely knew what *Pretty Woman* was even about). I felt mesmerized by Julia's fun-loving attitude and the fact that her style was always on point.

I also loved Disney movies, seeing as I was a 90's baby who had almost all the Disney VHS tapes. My favorites were *The Little Mermaid* and *Cinderella*—mostly because of my obsession with talking animals. I fantasized about the enchanted lands these princesses lived in and felt jealous of all the tiny critter friends that had their backs. When my real-life friends would come over, the first thing I'd suggest we do was reenact the plots from those movies.

At the time, Julia Roberts and talking animals may have been what drew me in, but those movies had one driving theme my five-year-old brain wasn't capable of recognizing: love. They depicted women whose lives changed forever the moment they fell in love. Since I was young and had nothing to go off of, my tiny prepubescent mind took notes from these stories as beliefs for how real life functioned.

Those videos I watched as a kid depicted love as something that alters a person's life for the best; essentially, romantic love makes life worth living. Giving up your life back home was a sensible trade-off; why swim with your sea creature friends and be able to see your family when you can have legs that lead you to a handsome man? If you're down and out because your father died or you ate a poison apple, love will be there to save you (I'm looking at you, Prince Charming). Those shiny VHS tapes in cases with gold borders sold us the idea that love at first sight is not only real, but the only kind of love that matters.

Like many people before and after me, the love I watched as a child in movies shaped my expectation of love as an adult. Of course, I didn't realize it for a while. I figured I was like any regular teenager if I wanted a boyfriend more than I cared to make friends. I believed my world would be rocked the moment I had my first boyfriend, and as a result, I ended up giving my heart to too many boys who weren't careful with it. I let men hurt me, again and again, for far too long because my notion of a loving relationship was far from accurate.

ALL OF US ARE PRESENTED WITH BELIEFS ABOUT LOVE WHEN WE'RE YOUNG, EVEN IF WE DON'T REALIZE IT.

It was in the plots of our favorite TV shows, the articles in magazines, and how our parents loved or didn't love each other. What you grew up to believe about love might be different from my beliefs or maybe you strongly related to my words above; either way, that's beside the point. Often, we have skewed ideas about how healthy love works and those end up being the reason we get into relationships with people who treat us badly or with whom we have little connection. We're blinded by the thought that we're on the path to writing the rest of the fairytale we saw when we were younger, only to be sorely disappointed when we realize love isn't quite like what we saw in movies.

There's no point in blaming anyone for any messed-up beliefs you picked up about love as a child. You can dwell on the realization that life was unfair and curse your parents or the media for imprinting these ideas into your innocent elementary school mind. Or you can do the work to create new beliefs on love. You can examine what your existing beliefs are, determine for yourself how you want your love life to look, and begin re-writing the narratives that aren't serving you anymore.

The moment you admit your beliefs surrounding love aren't creating the happiness you want, you're given the chance to change your entire perspective on it: not just romantic love, but platonic and self-love, too.

THE FIRST LOVE WE EXPERIENCE IN LIFE

From the moment we're born into this world, we begin forming a bond with the people who raise us. Our first loves will always be our parents, caregivers, and siblings, and the first model of romantic love will be the relationship our parents or caregivers had with each other. The affection and care they did or didn't show significantly affects the way we experience intimacy, love, and relationships today. Sometimes those effects are healthy and model a thriving relationship where both people effectively give and show love. But other times, that's not the case.

The research on this subject is extensive and one I'll reference throughout this book. From attachment style, to love languages, to "daddy issues," they're all linked back to how parents care for their children.

Some parents do a worse job than others or completely opt-out of their responsibility; if that was your case, I'm sorry you were dealt such a crappy hand in life. But most of the time, parents have good intentions, but their efforts fall short. No one is perfect, parents included. I'd consider my childhood in this latter category.

I don't have the happiest memories from my childhood. Sure, I remember traveling around the United States in our RV and getting a puppy when I was in middle school. I recall hanging out with friends in my neighborhood and excelling at school since the second grade. But what I don't have a lot of memories of is love.

My mom loved me; now that I'm an adult, she tells me she does, every chance she gets. I remember my mom being there for me when I needed her, though I grew to be an independent kid quickly. But for whatever reason, I never connected with her as a child and it's not easy to be close with her as an adult. I'm sure those two correlate with each other, and perhaps that's why I always struggled with female friendships. But now she tries to deepen our relationship and I give her credit for that.

My dad wasn't as great with his emotions. I know he cared in his own ways, but I don't ever recall my father saying I was beautiful or that he loved me when I was a child. Maybe he showed love in different ways, but it wasn't in a way I needed. When I was in high school, he had to move to California when he lost his job in my hometown in Florida. I was a sophomore at the time, but I remember him calling me twice, out of the two years he lived away from our family; both on my birthdays.

My brother is a whole other story; our relationship is non-existent. I don't have a single memory that doesn't involve him doing everything he could to keep me out of his life. It extended beyond the typical brother-sister fights of him yelling at me to get out of his room, to him chucking the remote at me if I made him mad. My mom said it was sibling rivalry and we'd grow out of it. We never did.

Not having a relationship with my brother stung; it wasn't easy seeing my friends be happily hanging out with their siblings when mine wanted nothing to do with me. By the time I got to middle school, I made a conscious effort to stop getting upset about the disappointment and pain my brother caused from how he treated me.

As a result of my childhood, I didn't form any strong, loving bonds with men in my life. Again, going back to the idea of "daddy issues," it's a fair assumption to believe my lack of connection with both my dad and brother affected my romantic relationships later in life. Those voids echo inside me, even today, and it took a lot of digging to realize how much my childhood affected my life as an adult.

While media and dating folklore greatly shapes the ways we think about love, there's no denying that how we're raised also greatly changes the way we experience love as adults. When your ability to bond with your parents or caregivers is disrupted, so is your entire sense of healthy, secure love.

I don't want you to make the realization that part of why you struggle with love is because of your childhood so that you can call up your parents and tell them what a crappy job they did. The past is in the past. There's no changing it now. But what you can do is work to uncover those wounds and move forward in a way that's not tethered to that childhood pain.

Again, this may sound like complete nonsense. You may be thinking, "How in the world could something that happened over a decade ago still be causing problems for me in my life?" The answer is long, so much so that people have written books on the subject. But I'll give you a short and sweet explanation of why your upbringing greatly affects your adulthood.

Humans are animals and like any other animal baby, we gain our understanding of the world from our parents. A bird learns to fly by watching its mom flap her wings and a human child learns to walk by observing their parents move their legs. This is the same reason why there are hilarious videos of one-year-olds saying "shit" as one of their first words; they didn't think of that word out of thin air. Those babies heard their parents curse whenever they stubbed their toe or forgot to pay the bills.

The same rule of babies learning from parents applies to love. The kind of love that your parents or caregivers showed for each other becomes your first example of how romantic relationships function. Unless someone drastically intervenes to change that narrative (or you do it yourself), you'll most likely grow up to act the same way in your relationships as your parents did.

Then there are the ways your parents interacted with you, shaping the way you can give and receive love. As a baby, you had needs: from a diaper change, to milk, to needing comfort when you were scared. Sometimes, caregivers are attentive, and are there whenever you need them. Other times, they're busy working or aren't equipped with the knowledge of how to properly care for a baby (because the reality is, it doesn't come naturally for everyone). Depending on which kind of care you received, you'll either form a secure or insecure attachment with your parents according to a popular study of psychology called attachment theory.

PEOPLE WITH A SECURE ATTACHMENT ARE THE ONES WHO NATURALLY THRIVE IN RELATIONSHIPS.

They rarely get jealous, can handle their emotions well, and balance their romantic life with their social life. On the other hand, people with an insecure attachment tend to be one of two things: anxious or avoidant. Anxious people (I'm one of them) tend to be the clingy, fearful type. We worry our partner will cheat or leave us at any moment. Over-thinking is our specialty. But on the flip side, the avoidantly attached types are usually the kind of people who fear commitment. They don't feel safe relying on others for emotional support, so they pull away. While it's not always the case that the way a parent raises their child leads to an insecure attachment, the chances are likely, which is why I decided to include attachment theory in this book.

Most people who struggle with dating and relationships (though not all) have some sort of insecure attachment. Don't get me wrong: modern dating is hard enough on its own. Everyone's living at a fast pace and looking for the next best thing; even secure people struggle because of the way that modern dating works. But having a less-than-stellar upbringing as a child will feel like other people got a twenty-second head start while you were tying your shoes.

Fear not, though. This realization isn't a death sentence for your love life. Rather, it's a chance to open your eyes to the realities of what you're dealing with. Instead of going into love blindly, you can understand yourself better and know why you act certain ways. One of the first steps to my journey of learning about love was reading the booked *Attached* and figuring out I have an anxious attachment. Instead of feeling bummed out, I felt relieved; someone put to words all the anxiety I'd felt for so long.

In life, there are a lot of things you can't change. The love you felt (or didn't feel) as a child is amongst them. But the beliefs you picked up because of your childhood? Those you do have a lot of control over. And what you read throughout this book will help you become more self-aware of your thoughts and beliefs, many of which will be a result of your childhood. You'll be asked to decide if certain ideas you have around love are no longer serving you. The exercises I mention will help you work past habits that no longer bring you happiness. But, most importantly, this book will help you realize you're not broken, and a lot of people are in the same boat as you. There are a lot of things you can do today to help shape your understanding of love and the ability to give and receive it with other people.

COMMON BELIEFS ABOUT LOVE, REFRAMED

||||||||||

"I believed; therefore, I was."

I've mentioned beliefs several times so far, so let's backtrack. What is a belief? It's something that's considered to be true by an individual. For example, I believe *Harry Potter* is a cinematic masterpiece. You, on the other hand, may think *Lord of The Rings* is better. While I think you're wrong (which is another belief), these are all just our ideas of what we believe to be true.

Every single one of us has beliefs about love. Just mentioning the word might elicit ideas you have about how much you love yourself, the people in your life, and any romantic partners you have or had. Those beliefs shape the way you experience and act in the world, trickling into the smallest crevices of your life. Beliefs about self-love changes your confidence, and how you love others affects your relationships.

From a very young age, I adopted a belief that I needed the approval of others to prove I was worth something. I was born in the suburbs of Orlando, in a town called Altamonte Springs. I lived in a condo with my older brother and parents. The arguing and my brother wanting nothing to do with me extended as far back as I can remember. I'd try hanging out in the pool when his friends came over to swim, but he always said he didn't want me around. I attempted to get him to play games with me outside, but my efforts were met with insults. The only happy memories I have is a photo of my brother and I sitting on top of his bunk bed when I was three and he was six. My mom said we used to ask to sleep together all the time and we looked elated in that photo, holding his Power Ranger action figures. But I was too young to remember that night, so the picture feels like a foreign memory that didn't happen to me but to someone who looked like me.

Things between my brother and I only got worse as we grew up. The mere idea of me entering his room filled him with rage. I remember a time when I needed to go into his room to grab his garbage can so I could empty it as part of my chores, and he tried to hit me as he yelled to get out. Everyone brushed it off as two siblings who "didn't get along," but it's been twenty years and things aren't different.

The fact my brother wanted nothing to do with me hurt, but I focused on those whose approval I could obtain: my parents. I started doing everything I could to be great at school so my parents would take notice. Color inside the lines? You've got it; here's my drawing that went on to win the art fair for all the kindergarten classes at my school. Learn to read? I had *The Magic Treehouse* down by the time I hit second grade.

Sure, from this, a healthy competitive spirit grew inside me (although I hate losing, so maybe not *that* healthy). But at the same time, I functioned too closely off the belief that if I excelled at something, my parents would love me more. Not only that, but other people like my friends and grandma would love me more, too. I realized if I changed myself, whether it be my performance at school or my obsession with my weight I later acquired, I could gain people's admiration and attention, if only for the time being.

Obviously, that's not a very healthy way to function. Chasing the affection of others isn't a stable way to live. But once I had those beliefs, it took a lot of work to undo them.

Your beliefs can guide you through living a life that's true to your morals and helps you feel authentic in everything you do. Or they can be what limits and holds you back from that same life.

Limiting beliefs tend to hold some truth because we don't form them out of nowhere. At some point in our lives, we latched onto certain ideas because of the situations we experienced. You may believe all people will hurt you because a parent left when you were young. For me, I thought love had to be earned from my parents, and I could make sure they wouldn't change their minds if I worked hard enough. But the lie one experience tells you can end up affecting the rest of your life. That is, until you decide to do something about it.

BELIEFS SURROUNDING LOVE EXTEND BEYOND OUR NOTIONS OF ROMANCE; THEY AFFECT EVERY RELATIONSHIP WE EXPERIENCE THROUGHOUT OUR LIVES.

You might already be aware of the beliefs you have, or maybe you're completely new to questioning your subconscious ideas about life. Wherever you are on your journey, you're exactly where you're meant to be.

I've found, through talking with friends, answering reader's questions, and doing my own research, that there are many common beliefs people have about love. If any of the following limiting beliefs resonate with you, as a small exercise, try re-framing these beliefs.

REFRAMING LIMITING BELIEFS ABOUT LOVE

Limiting belief: "I am broken."
Re-frame: "I've been through pain but so has everyone. That does not make me less lovable."

Limiting belief: "I'm not worthy of love."
Re-frame: "I am worthy of beautiful things in life, including love."

Limiting belief: "Everyone will break my heart."
Re-frame: "Someone hurt me in the past but that does not mean everyone will."

Limiting belief: "Being alone is scary."
Re-frame: "Being alone is a chance to make changes in my life that will bring me the happiness I desire."

Limiting belief: "I cannot trust people."
Re-frame: "I will try to trust people until they give me a reason not to."

Limiting belief: "I must change to be worthy of love."
Re-frame: "I know I am worthy of love and there is plenty in the world for me."

Limiting belief: "Everyone will eventually leave."
Re-frame: "The people meant to be in my life will stay."

Limiting belief: "My love is too much for people."

Re-frame: "My love isn't too much, I've just been giving it to the wrong people."

Limiting belief: "Everything is going wrong."
Re-frame: "Everything is going the way it needs to go."

Limiting belief: "I need a relationship to complete me."
Re-frame: "I am whole on my own and a relationship is just a bonus."

Limiting belief: "I need a perfect relationship."
Re-frame: "I need someone who is willing to learn how to love me in the ways I need."

Limiting belief: "I'm selfish for doing what I want."
Re-frame: "By being the happiest version of myself, I show up better for others."

Limiting belief: "There's something wrong with me for being single."
Re-frame: "I am not the problem. A great relationship comes in its own time."

Limiting belief: "Love will save me."
Re-frame: "I will save me."

LIES SOCIETY TELLS US ABOUT LOVE THAT YOU SHOULD IGNORE

||||||||||

"Once you wake up to the realities of life, that not everything you've been told is true or permanent, you won't be able to go back to sleep."

I've had plenty of people lie to me. Family, whether it be to keep me from getting hurt or making themselves look bad. Friends, about their intentions for being my friend (*cough*, Sarah from middle school who dated my neighbor and would sleep over so she could sneak out to meet him). Boyfriends, in every sense of the idea that boyfriends can lie to you.

And while those lies hurt to find out about, the myths society feeds us about love ended up impacting me far beyond any lie one person told me. I mean, they're the entire reason I'm writing this book. These lies shaped the way I experienced love up until the very day I stopped believing them, which I'll get more into later.

You probably bought into these lies, too; until we question them, there's no reason to think they couldn't possibly be true. They were weaved into magazine articles with titles like "How to Get a Man So You Can End Your Tragic Single Life." Movies like

Pretty Woman (how could you, Julia) instilled them in us by watching Edward swoop into Vivian's life like a knight in shining armor.

And we weren't the first generation this has happened to. Our parents before us were fed similar lies, and their parents before them. And it's no surprise that no one realizes the harm they do; people pass down those lies from generation to generation, mother to daughter to sister, like a truth no one questions.

That is, until now. I'm bringing up the most prevalent lies about love because they weave little roots into many aspects of our lives and wreak havoc. These lies aren't just misguided, wrong, and often ridiculous, but they're ideas you should ignore if you ever come across them:

BEING TOO INDEPENDENT WILL KEEP YOU FROM LOVE

When I took a year-long break from dating, I wanted to uncover why I relied so heavily on the men I dated; not just for helping me build Ikea furniture, but for emotional needs, too. I went so deep into the work of becoming an independent woman I started to feel like I was heading in the wrong direction. "I'm going to become one of those women who kicks ass at her job and no guy wants to be with," I thought, which I'm embarrassed to even admit.

The truth is, the best kind of relationship is where two people having thriving lives outside of their relationship. Whether that looks like working hard at your career, seeing your friends every week, or pursuing your passions intensely, independence should be celebrated. If someone is scared off by your happiness in life, then good riddance.

THAT YOUR PARTNER SHOULD BE YOUR "RIDE OR DIE"

Anyone who tells you that you should stay in a relationship no matter what is doing more harm than good. I've been in situations where I was emotionally abused and those impacts greatly affected my mental health for years to come. But instead of leaving them, I thought I should stay; that somehow, we'd work things out.

The moment someone breaks your trust in a way you can't forgive, or hurts you physically, emotionally, or sexually, you need to consider if the relationship is worth keeping. Don't automatically buy into the notion you'll work through all the bad times; that's only perpetuating that idea the other person can mistreat you. Sometimes, standing by your partner will put you in the way of danger. Those are the times you need to leave.

YOU CAN'T BE SINGLE AND HAPPY

I used to think I needed to date until I found "the one." I couldn't be happy unless I was in a relationship, so why would I stop to take a break? But when I chose to take that one-year hiatus from dating, I surprised myself by creating a life in which I was happily single. I didn't need love from another person to make me happy; I could build a life that gave that love to me instead.

I can't stress enough that your happiness is not determined by your love life. All those movies where women are insatiably miserable while single got one thing right: the mindset of the main characters sucked and was actually the issue. Instead of believing singledom marks you as problematic, you should use that time to do things that bring you happiness.

MEN NEED TO BE THE STRONG ONES

We're lucky to live in a time where this notion is being questioned, but even today, fathers pass down to their sons the belief they need to bottle up their feelings. Then those same guys get into relationships and think they need to be emotionless and strong for their women. But that belief is antiquated and, for people who date men, won't bring you a healthy relationship if you buy into that notion, too. So, while men should strive for emotional vulnerability, women should also encourage the same in the men they date.

A relationship is symbiotic. You take, you give. Your partner takes, they give. The role of the "strong one" will fluctuate throughout the lifetime of a relationship, no matter who it is you're dating.

LOVE IS A FEELING

I once read a graphic on Instagram (of course) that explained the best way to deal with harmful thought spirals is remembering that feelings are fleeting. You'll only feel sad about someone not texting you back if you give that thought your energy. When you do something else to refocus your mind, that melancholy feeling disappears.

That's because feelings aren't permanent. So, love can't possibly be a feeling. If it were, it would mean monogamy and long-lasting relationships wouldn't exist. At least, not beyond some type of financial or status gain. What I've come to realize is lust and passion are often mistaken for love. But love is what's left of a relationship after all the pretty parts fall away and the puppy love passes. It's why someone can drive you crazy one day but be your favorite person the next. It's why sometimes, love is hard and won't always be perfect.

Love is more of a choice. At the end of the day, you still choose one another.

LOVE WILL SAVE YOU

It's a classic trope that a woman will be saved from her cursed life by Prince Charming. Even nowadays, you'll come across people who think they're your gift from heaven.

While a relationship can support you through your struggles, it won't be what saves you.

I thought I had to present my broken pieces to my partner to see if they loved me. Now I realize I don't have to be broken to be loved and it's not my partner's responsibility to fix me.

Love will not save you. Only you can save yourself.

PART II

MOVING PAST HEARTBREAK

YOU CAN'T MAKE SOMEONE CHOOSE YOU

ııııııııı

"Matters of the heart aren't something you can control. People love who they love. That can either be a beautiful truth, or your greatest suffering."

I dated my first semi-serious boyfriend, which I base on the fact my parents actually knew he existed, during my sophomore year of high school. His name was Travis, and I was drawn to the fact he was in a rock band: different from the stereotypical jock I was normally attracted to. Sure, he was in the school band, too, which, at the time, I was too self-absorbed to see as anything beyond dorky. But he balanced it out by performing at venues with his band on the weekends.

Travis was the son of my mom's best friend. We've known each other since we were both in diapers and drooling on ourselves (a very cute first impression). Our moms took us to the local zoo and Kennedy Space Center together, along with our other siblings. I'd never thought anything more of Travis than the fact he was my mom's friend's son I was forced to hang out with as a kid.

During a BBQ that Travis's mom threw during my sophomore year of high school, I noticed a slight flirtation forming in the way Travis talked to me. "You know what, he's kind of cute," I thought to myself while I examined his charming smile. After that day, a sudden shift happened: we started making plans together, rather than our moms forcing us to see each other. One day, while Travis and I laid on the floor of his bedroom watching *Tomb Raider*, I felt his hand reach out to hold mine. I thought to myself, "Well if this isn't the making of an epic love story, I don't know what is."

Travis's bad-boy vibe mixed with his endearing personality had me enamored. We'd walk around school, hands always clasped together. We spent our weekends hauling his guitars and amps in my car to local venues around Orlando. Looking back, I was basically a groupie but with girlfriend status, which I didn't mind. In fact, I loved being with him so much that I didn't care that I spent my Friday night in bars with people covered in tattoos and head-banging to people screaming.

Six months into our relationship, I started to feel Travis pull away from me. He began hanging out with a group of girls from his band class more than he did with me, which weirded me out, but I tried to play it cool. When I asked him what was up with his newfound friend group, Travis wrote off my question as me being possessive. He never invited me to the plans their group made, never introduced me aside from the fact I had marine biology with two of the girls.

One day, after Travis promised to meet me at my car after school and didn't show up, I went looking for him. Again, he was with the same group of girls. I walked up to him to ask why he ditched me, and he immediately started yelling at me for being needy. "I just want my space!" he said while the people he was talking to stood there watching. I was shocked. Not only was the whole situation humiliating, but I felt betrayed by someone I felt close to. I walked away in tears and later that night, Travis called to break up with me.

Soon after, a rumor started spreading around our school: Travis, a senior at the time, was getting involved with a freshman who, you might've guessed, was part of that same group of girls he'd recently befriended. I was blindsided; the girl was his little sister's age. Imagining the two of them together, kissing in the band room, and laughing at the idea of Travis yelling at me, made me feel queasy. My mind raced to wondering how long something might've been going on between them. This rumor shocked me; the mere thought of it being true felt like Travis took my heart and smashed it with his guitar.

A few weeks passed and that rumor died down. In fact, Travis texted me one day asking if I could drive him home so we could talk about "us." Turned out, he wanted to give things between me and him another shot. I felt elated. I'd been secretly hoping Travis would change his mind about dating since the moment we broke up. Later that day while driving Travis home, I focused on the road ahead of me, but all I wanted to do was wrap my arms around him. When I pulled up at his house, we shared a beautiful kiss that made everything feel as though it were back to normal.

On my way home, I heard a vibration coming from the side of my car. It sounded like a phone but mine was laying on my seat. When I got to my house, I searched the side of the passenger seat and found that Travis left his phone in my car. Being the sixteen-year-old girl I was, I checked the messages he received while I was driving home. Low and behold, they were from the freshman girl Travis claimed he stopped seeing. Not only was he still talking to her, but it seemed like he never even tried to stop.

After giving Travis his phone back the next day, he went back to being defensive; as if our talk about getting back together never happened. He ignored my pleas for him to stop talking to the other girl and again, he defended his stance that we couldn't be together. I couldn't convince Travis to choose me. The aftermath of that conversation was a mixture of feeling rejected and crazy. I thought Travis and I would have a fairytale ending since we'd known each other for so long; I mean, our moms were best friends. It seemed like a no-brainer.

The pain I experienced after that breakup felt like it would last a lifetime. I can't say I truly got over Travis until my second year of college (probably because we had a few flings in between). But the fact is, I was never the girl Travis chose to be with. Now I realize Travis wasn't the bad guy.

I thought I loved Travis at the time. I thought since I loved him, he should love me back in the same way. I thought, through the power of convincing and sheer will power, I could make Travis love me. I could be the one he chose.

BUT WHEN SOMEONE'S HEART IS ELSEWHERE, YOU CAN'T CHANGE THAT FOR THEM.

You might have the urge to convince someone why you work so well together, but love (or infatuation, lust, chemistry, whatever it is) doesn't work logically. We can't explain or control who we feel it for.

There are many people in your life who will choose you: friends, family, a crush, or that one person you never considered dating but are realizing they're pretty cute. Invest your energy into those people actively wanting to be a part of your life, not someone you have to convince to love you. A convinced love will never feel as good as you dream it will. Especially when there are plenty of people out there who will choose you without thinking twice.

LESSONS YOU CAN LEARN FROM ANY BREAKUP

||||||||||

"Remember:
Not everyone will embrace your light.
Not everyone will make room.
Not everyone will want what's best for you."

When I was 19, I transferred from my college in Florida to the university my dad worked at in Los Angeles: a foreign but alluring city that felt extremely overwhelming. I'd seen California on TV and even visited my dad once while he waited for my mom to sell our house back in Florida. But living in Los Angeles was a whole different ball game. Everyone was beautiful, ambitious, and trying to be famous.

After a year of living in LA and working as a hostess at The Cheesecake Factory, a co-worker asked me to help him with a short film he was producing. He needed a blonde woman for one of the roles, and I agreed to take the part. On the day of the table read for my co-worker's project, a guy walked into the room wearing dark jeans, a white tee, and perfectly messy hair. He caught my eye the second I saw him, and apparently, the feeling was mutual.

His name was Sean, and he was an actor/model in the city. We grabbed lunch at an Asian fusion restaurant the following day to get to know one another, and that meal ended with us making out in my Honda Civic in the parking garage of the Century City Mall.

Everything after our first date felt like a whirlwind. We started seeing each other almost every day: mostly at my place, because Sean was couch surfing at the time. A few weeks into dating, he took me to Huntington Beach to meet his mom and teach me to surf. While we were out on the ocean, Sean looked up at me with an adoring smile. "I love you," he said. I splashed ocean water toward him and joked, "you don't know what love is." The next week, we decided he would move in with me.

Our love was probably the annoying kind you see in movies; we were obsessed with each other. We did all the usual puppy love stuff: baby talking in public and sitting on the same side of the table. I'm sure we made the poor souls around us queasy. But we were in love; we were as happy as a couple could be. At least for a bit.

Half a year into our relationship, I started noticing things suddenly shifting. Sean went from being an adoring boyfriend who would leave me love notes in the bathroom to a man who criticized me over a single crumb on the kitchen counter. Sean's doting comments turned into insults about how much fat I held in my arms or how thoughtless I was for forgetting to make the bed. He started to convince me my friends weren't good influences, and I believed him, slowly removing people from my life one by one. Our picture-perfect romance turned into a narrative of Sean telling me he deserved to date someone who was as beautiful as the models he worked with.

Instead of leaving Sean, I internalized every word that came from his mouth. I started to question my own sanity. I wondered how I even got into college, believing Sean's words that I was stupid and careless. He convinced me his shady behaviors—pretending he was single so famous actresses would potentially hang out with him and flirting with his manager to get auditions—were just part of show biz. Even the way he'd yell at his mom and pick fights with his stepdad was always followed by excuses that seemed reasonable.

Sean and I dated for two years, and even though I became a mere shell of the person I used to be, I loved him. When he broke up with me while we were on a road trip, it felt like I'd lost half of who I was. Our lives were entangled, and I couldn't imagine how I'd live without him.

If you're in the midst of heartbreak, I know it feels impossible to look past your present life when it's been drastically altered. I'm all too familiar with the pain of someone important to you—even if they weren't good for you—removing themselves from your life. It's like a part of your heart is torn off and placed as an uneasy presence in your stomach. I won't sit here and lie about how a breakup isn't shattering.

But when the time comes that you can breathe a bit easier, when the tears stop showing up as often, I want to challenge you to see your breakup as something more than pain. Every person that comes into your life does so for a reason. That doesn't mean they'll always stay; far from it, actually. Some people will come into your life only for a moment; others will stay years before they leave.

But after each departure, you'll have an opportunity to reflect. I want to challenge you to look back on your relationships and figure out what they can teach you. A lesson doesn't always come wrapped neatly in a glossy paper with an ornate bow. Sometimes, they're messy and hard to decipher. But if you're open to realizing the lesson learned from your heartbreak, you'll be better off in preparing yourself for future encounters with love.

The following are several lessons that may be waiting for you to learn after a breakup:

WHAT YOU DON'T WANT IN A RELATIONSHIP

At the very least, a breakup will always be a chance to learn what you don't want in a relationship. Everything that annoyed or rubbed you the wrong way about your ex, make note of those; write them down, even. Consider why you never felt comfortable in their presence. Question if you had to change part of yourself to fit their morals/standards/values or vice versa.

If you don't stop to consider what you didn't like in your past relationships, you won't know what to look for in future ones.

YOU CAN'T CHANGE SOMEONE

Change is a tall order for anyone, even more so when the pressure is coming from an external source (aka, you). If you wanted your partner to change, but they didn't agree with you, it's probably the reason the change never happened.

Asking someone to alter who they are is a significant request. Really, for anyone to want to change, they need to want it for themselves, deep down. If you think simply asking someone to be different so you can both be happier is a solution, you'll most often be disappointed. The bright side to this realization is that there is someone out there who you won't feel the need to change.

UNHEALTHY LOVE EXISTS

This lesson was the hardest for me to learn. I'd been blinded by the love I felt for Sean so much so that I ignored how unhealthy we were together. I mean, if you're in love, that's all a relationship needs to succeed, right?

The reality is, you can love someone and still not be healthy for each other. I've realized that's true, in romance and all relationships in life. When you can't be the best version of yourself with someone, you end up causing yourself a lot of anxiety and pain. Passion might feel like enough to create a loving relationship but you need respect, maturity, and willingness to work on things to create something that has the potential to last.

YOU CAN SURVIVE ANYTHING

Your heart may be heavy now, but one day it will lighten. One day the world will feel a bit less cold and you'll start to reawaken to the possibilities of life being different, that you'll move on from this.

When that time comes, look back on the moment you thought you wouldn't make it through this breakup. Remember how you felt deeply consumed by this moment in your life and smile now that you've made it through. Because weathering a breakup is painful. If you can come out of one having learned and grown, you can survive anything.

MOVING ON IS THE BEST REVENGE

||||||||||

"The best gift your ex will ever give you is leaving. In the end, you don't want to waste your time with someone who would choose to spend theirs without you."

I remember the first time I heard Carrie Underwood's *Before He Cheats*. My mom was driving to the grocery store and she turned up the volume; she was a big *American Idol* fan. When the verse got to Carrie keying her ex's "pretty little souped up four-wheel-drive," my mom sighed. "Trying to terrorize your ex is the worst way to get revenge. Just move on and be happy; that will cause them more pain."

When someone hurts you, it's natural to want to hurt them back, especially when it comes to relationships. But before you pick up those car keys—I mean this emotionally, not physically. Just because you broke up doesn't mean all your feelings suddenly disappeared. A breakup can stir up a lot of emotions for people like anger and self-pity. If your heart was broken by someone else, letting go of your attachment to those feelings means letting go of the relationship entirely. It's hard to feel ready for that.

But my mom's wise words still ring true: the best revenge you can take on an ex is moving on with your life.

During the winter break of my senior year in college, Sean and I took a road trip from Los Angeles to Seattle. On the last day of our trip, we got into a horrible fight and broke up (with six hours of driving left, mind you). That trip magnified every issue in our relationship, and we argued without mercy. Sean hated that I wasn't good at planning and I resented him for sleeping in until 1 pm and consistently threatening to take a plane ride home. Finally, as we drove back to Los Angeles in near silence, Sean decided he'd use that opportunity to end our relationship. That last six hours was pure torture.

Since the breakup wasn't my idea, I did whatever I could to keep Sean in my life. I offered for him to stay living in my apartment and even keep sleeping in my bed. The idea of free rent was an offer he jumped at. He teetered on the line of acting like my boyfriend, but with zero commitment. The night he came home to tell me he'd made out with a famous actress (from my favorite TV show at the time, double blow), I realized what a jerk he was and that he only cared about himself. I wanted him to feel the same pain he'd made me feel for years.

I downloaded dating apps and started going on dates with other guys. I flirted with Sean's friends when we all went out to bars. I acted like I wasn't fazed by the breakup when, inside, I was a total wreck.

My attempts at revenge kept backfiring on me; it was like trying to put a tiny bandage on a gaping wound and being like, "yep, it'll heal on its own." The dates I tried going on didn't make me feel better, if anything the weird personalities of the guys I met made me miss Sean more. Flirting with Sean's friends got me essentially nowhere; I either looked dumb when they weren't interested, or I was in an awkward position if they did flirt back. And trying to make Sean feel my emotional pain backfired since he basically had no emotions (at least that he displayed).

Luckily, I had the end of college to distract me. It wasn't until my final semester at college when I started thinking about what I would do after. Being in a crappy relationship and balancing a job at the same time left me little room to think about what I wanted my career to be for the rest of my life. Actually, I'd always had this wild idea of moving abroad; seeing the world for myself, and finding random jobs to make ends meet. The idea of staying in Los Angeles, where Sean would always be, felt like too much to handle, so I started to search for options on how I could work abroad. I wanted Sean out of my life, once and for all, and a different continent seemed like enough space. So, I ran away as any person would, but I did it a bit differently.

Dramatic? Yes. Necessary? Definitely not. A bit irresponsible? You bet. But I'm grateful I was in the position to find a job abroad and not dive into a career straight out of college. A day hasn't passed where I regretted that decision.

I moved to Chengdu, China a month after I received my diploma. The day I packed up my suitcases and moved across the world to Asia was the moment I got my ultimate revenge. I was free of Sean. I simply moved on with my life. It might have been a dramatic choice—I'm certainly not implying you need to move to the other side of the world to get over your ex—but I knew there was more for me out there than being stuck in my resentment toward Sean.

I wasted one too many months thinking revenge was the way I'd get over Sean. I thought the answer was to make him feel the same kind of pain he caused me. But all it did was prolong the time it took me to move on with my life.

Whether you're posting a thirst trap on your Instagram because you hope your ex will see it or trying to sabotage their new relationship, that kind of revenge on your ex will never give you the satisfaction you crave. The energy you invest into an old relationship only ends up draining you. A grudge against your ex has a very lonely population of one.

Lingering in your resentment might feel like the right choice at the time, but what you're actually doing is continuing your pain. If you're honest with yourself, I'm sure you'd agree this person doesn't deserve an ounce more of your energy, so why waste more on them?

REST ASSURED THAT IF YOUR EX MEANT TO HURT YOU, THEIR TIME WILL COME

No one moves through this world causing others pain without eventually finding themselves in the same place. You don't need to take out revenge on them, the universe will eventually catch up to their ways.

FOCUS INSTEAD ON YOURSELF

Try to love yourself more than you ever loved them (more on this in the next section). Channel your energy into acts of love instead of revenge. Go for a walk and enjoy the feeling of the sun's rays on your skin. Spend time connecting with friends you lost touch with during your relationship. Enjoy the activities you stopped doing because your ex didn't support them.

PUT WORDS TO THE EMOTIONS YOU EXPERIENCE

When you think of breakups, you might imagine enraged women or pissed off men hitting the wall and yelling at their ex. Well, if you're feeling the same, it might come as a shock to you that you're probably not experiencing anger. Often, people use anger as a filler emotion; what we really feel is betrayed, sad, scared, or confused. Figuring out what you're feeling can help you cool down in situations where you feel overwhelmed. For me, saying things out loud like, "I'm feeling hurt because I trusted my ex," helped during the worst parts of my breakups.

OF COURSE, TAKE AS MUCH TIME YOU NEED TO GRIEVE

No one can set a marker on how long it takes to get over a breakup. It's a process you have to go through at your own pace. But moving through your feelings is different than clinging to parts of the relationship in an attempt to somehow keep what you once had alive.

WHEN THE TIME COMES THAT YOU'RE READY TO MOVE ON, YOU'LL BE TAKING YOUR ULTIMATE REVENGE

You'll let go of living in a place where you hope your ex will see the error of their ways because the reality is, they might never do so, but that doesn't mean the pain they caused you wasn't real. It doesn't mean you should wait for them to apologize. Sever the attachment you had with them and move into a life that doesn't include them. Because this, my friend, is the ultimate revenge. Nothing feels worse than watching someone you thought would break rise up into a stronger version of themselves.

A FEW DIFFICULT TRUTHS ON LOVE

||||||||||

"Love is realizing you have all the power to hurt someone but choosing not to. Not the other way around."

In your lifetime, you'll hear some version of the idea "love is what makes life worth living," if you haven't already. Movies show women giving up everything for a man who will love them. Magazines depict relationships as a game to win and the ultimate prize is the giant-stuffed-bear-equivalent of being in love. Popular culture tends to depict a certain kind of relationship; one that makes you feel a lot of emotions in the moment, like when Vivian is finally "rescued" by Edward in *Pretty Woman*. But if you want a healthy relationship, this kind of love is not what you want to strive for.

These notions that love is the pinnacle of a woman's life can cloud your judgment. Putting love on a pedestal might be keeping you from understanding what healthy love is and what it isn't.

Like anything, my relationship with Sean, the college beau, wasn't black and white. I can't look back and parse out the healthy from the unhealthy, or the good from the bad—although I could write a novel on the terrible. Because the fact is, we had plenty of great times. We spent many late nights sitting on my couch while he quizzed me with flashcards for my Native American Studies final. Sean helped me up from the snow whenever I fell while he taught me to snowboard. He supported me through the death of my grandfather, something I've only ever been through with him.

But I also can't neglect the parts that snuck up on me. Like when we argued, he threatened to get in his car, leave, and disappear out of my life. I'd cry enough tears for him to change his mind, and then the cycle would continue. Sean liked to find my weakness; he'd shred my confidence down by telling me I should skip a meal because of how big I looked that day.

And while I can see now that I cried more than I ever laughed, at the time, I thought that was how love worked. Forming an intimate connection with someone isn't easy for me, and I couldn't fathom letting Sean go after becoming so close to him. But I only fought what needed to eventually happen.

They say love is one of the best things to happen to us, and that's true. But you'll only find that kind of love after you accept several difficult truths.

CONSTANT STRUGGLE AND TEARS AREN'T LOVE

Somewhere along the way you might've mistaken pain for passion and therefore love. I was in the same position. If I wasn't fighting with a boyfriend, I assumed we lacked the fireworks everyone talked about. But what I never stopped to consider was that drama is not in fact, love.

Because love shouldn't hurt; it shouldn't leave you crying on the floor of your bathroom. Those feelings of intense fear that someone will leave you aren't love, they're an obsession. And being obsessed with anyone in life won't end well for you—unless it's yourself. Love is when the good outweighs the bad, not the other way around.

YOU CAN'T FORCE SOMEONE TO LOVE YOU

Imagine a food you're not fond of. How much forcing would someone have to do for you to change your mind? There probably isn't an amount because no one can magically change your distaste for a certain food. The same goes for love and whether someone feels it for you.

If someone doesn't love you, you can't force them to change their mind. If they don't want to be in your life, eventually, they will make their way out of it. You can either cause yourself more distress by standing in their way or move aside to let them leave.

LOVE ISN'T ENOUGH TO MAKE A RELATIONSHIP WORK

Relationships aren't a simple recipe; they're like a complex soufflé. There are not two steps to make one, but rather a multitude of ingredients and instructions that need to happen in a certain order to work.

Just like you can't make soufflé out of only an egg, you can't make a relationship only with chemistry. You need other ingredients like trust, respect, vulnerability, and quality time together. If a relationship lacks most of the ingredients, chemistry cannot make up for them. The relationship won't rise.

PEOPLE WILL ALWAYS MAKE TIME FOR THE THINGS THEY WANT IN THEIR LIFE

If someone takes forever to text you back or never makes plans to hang out, you're not a priority in their life. That's a tough truth to swallow, but it's simply how people work.

Think of a person in your life who loves working out. They go to the gym almost every day, no matter what. The same goes for dating and relationships. If someone is flaky, they're indifferent about following through on their plans with you. Because if they wanted to see you, they would. And the chances of that ever changing are very slim.

YOU CAN'T FILL YOUR LACK OF SELF-LOVE WITH SOMEONE ELSE'S AFFECTION

Another's love will never be enough to replace your own. Repeat that sentence to yourself as many times as you need to for it to sink in.

When you aren't happy about who you are, your insecurities will hold you back. A relationship won't magically fix the parts of your life you hate. I, for instance, felt insecure about my looks and my intelligence. I ended up leaning on Sean to fill those voids (and you saw how well that turned out). Your insecurities will only be magnified when they're tested by your relationship.

YOU DON'T NEED TO BE BROKEN TO BE DESERVING OF LOVE

If you've ever gone through a painful experience or time in your life, you might start to think something is wrong with you, like you're broken. I felt the same, and I thought I needed to present those broken parts of myself to my boyfriends and have them put the pieces back together. That process, I thought, was how love formed.

It took a long time to realize that's not how love works and, more importantly, I'm not broken. I'm merely a sum of everything that happened in my past, and so are you. No matter what you've been through, you're still deserving of respect and love.

HOW TO TELL IF YOU'RE WITH THE WRONG PERSON

||||||||||

"And when you ignore your instincts, a bit of you compromises; a bit of you withers away. Because someone who ignores the truth that aches to be realized is a person who surrenders to a life half-lived."

For over the past decade, I've been in one relationship after another. I've told a total of eight men I loved them. Yet today, I'm only with one of those men.

I'm not stating that fact to brag. If anything, my serial monogamy did more harm than good because I deserve to take a moment to be single and just breathe. But one thing's for sure: I have a lot of experience being with the wrong person.

I imagined several different future weddings with men I thought were "the one." Depending on the person, I'd daydream about our vineyard wedding and how their faces would look when they saw me walking down the aisle. If we were more serious, I'd think about what it would be like having children with them and growing old. What can I say? I've always been a hopeless romantic.

But now, those plans feel like silly, distant memories. While I don't regret any of my relationships, because there's always a lesson to learn from any relationship, I wish I would've left some of my relationships sooner. Because, if I was being honest with myself, I knew a lot of my relationships didn't make me happy. And the signs were, many times, obvious but I ignored them in favor of focusing on the good.

To figure out if you're with the wrong person, you have to do a few things first:

- **Be honest with yourself.** Most of the time, people know they're with the wrong person; they're just scared to admit it. No matter how many articles or books you read, you won't be able to reassure yourself enough to make up for the courage you need to admit that things aren't working.

- **Take off the rose-colored glasses.** Don't try to only see the good in your partner; take note of the bad as well. Better yet, see what they present to you (their actions, more so than words) and take them at face value. Don't make excuses for someone who doesn't deserve them.

- **Have tough conversations.** There will be issues in any relationship you get into. Maybe what's bothering you is something your partner hasn't realized about themself. It's OK to be honest with them about where your head is at. Plus, learning to have tough conversations will help you grow.

If you're able to do the above with yourself, then you'll be in the right headspace to figure out if you're with the wrong person. Through my seven failed relationships I thought would last forever, I noticed there are several key moments to realizing someone isn't the person for you.

SILENT MOMENTS FEEL AWKWARD

This is such a small, seemingly insignificant part of a relationship, but feeling awkward when you and your partner aren't talking isn't a great sign. It means you're uncomfortable being in their presence. If silence makes you feel like you need to quickly think of something to say, I'd ask yourself how comfortable you feel in your relationship.

YOU FEEL LIKE YOU NEED A LOT OF SPACE

If you both work from home and you want space, that's healthy. If you want to see your friends for a night, without your partner, then go out and have fun. But if every night, you're wishing you could just be alone or that your partner wasn't around, ask yourself if you're just very independent, or if you aren't happy in your relationship anymore.

THEIR OPINIONS MAKE YOU FEEL UNCOMFORTABLE

I used to date a man who I now realize was sexist and racist. The things he said made my skin crawl. While I was bothered by his comments at the time, I forgot about his words shortly after he said them. I kept quiet and let his horrible remarks slide. But doing that meant I wasn't acknowledging how wildly different our morals and values were. His comments were waving red flags that I wasn't with the right person.

YOUR NEEDS FEEL INCOMPATIBLE

Only you know what bothers you to the point that you feel upset. It may be something as little as you wanting to text throughout the day, but your partner never checks their phone. Or maybe you love to talk about your emotions, but your partner sees feelings as a sign of weakness. These kinds of differences aren't small; they're a sign your needs aren't being met.

YOU DON'T FEEL RESPECTED

With any relationship in your life, romantic or platonic, you need to feel respected. A healthy relationship means both people are seen as equals by each other, instead of one person being put up on a pedestal. Disrespect is a clear sign you're with someone who doesn't treat you well. Eventually, you'll grow to resent them.

YOU REGULARLY DREAM OF A DIFFERENT LIFE

After I graduated college and moved abroad to China, I dated a British guy (I'll get into more details later). We weren't together for long before I started dreaming of living elsewhere and figuring out what life had to offer. The problem? Those fantasies never included my boyfriend. It's clear today I didn't see a future with him. I only saw a "for now" between us (which I don't regret).

YOU FEEL ISOLATED FROM THE REST OF YOUR LIFE

Whether your partner keeps you from your life outside of the relationship, or you feel obligated to spend all your time with them, neither of these are healthy signs. A supportive partner will encourage you to see your friends and pursue hobbies. A thriving relationship will be one where you live individual lives that you choose to share together.

YOU FEEL TRAPPED

If your relationship makes you feel trapped, it's time to start making a game plan for how to leave. It's not OK to feel like you're unwillingly choosing your relationship. Being with another person is a choice you can either make or not. But if you're feeling stuck, both of you deserve to be with someone else.

YOU CAN'T IMAGINE SPENDING YOUR LIFE WITH THEM

Once you've been with someone long enough, you can usually get a sense of whether you can see the relationship lasting. If, right off the bat, thinking about "forever" makes you feel claustrophobic, then that's not a good sign. I'm not saying you have to commit to "forever" right now, but not being able to picture a future at all is something to consider.

Don't get me wrong, there's always value in every relationship you have. And just because a relationship doesn't last forever doesn't mean it was a waste of time.

But if you want a serious relationship, and you're in one that feels like it's going nowhere or isn't making you happy, then ask yourself if you're with the wrong person. You both deserve to move on and find someone who you enjoy being with more.

WAYS TO CARE FOR YOURSELF AFTER A BREAKUP

||||||||||

"If there's one thing I hope for you, it's this: I hope you wake up one day, look in the mirror, and see what everyone who cares for you sees. Someone who made it through the thick of the worst. Someone who not only found their way out but emerged stronger, ready for anything. I hope you feel the same sense of awe that others in your life experience when in your presence. I hope you see the eyes of the person who stumbled, hurt, and bled. But in those same eyes, you see a person who chose humility, asked for help, and refused to let fear hold them back."

I won't deny that breakups are hard; having your heart broken feels like your world is shaken to its core. Your everyday life suddenly changes and the loss of someone important to you can feel like you lost part of yourself.

After being a serial monogamist for over a decade, I've been through quite a few heartbreaks. Every time a relationship ended,

I tried the usual ways of moving on: going out with friends, talking to someone new, or the all-too-cliché texting my ex. In fact,
my first time downloading a dating app was because I wanted to
get out of my apartment (which I shared with an ex).

But instead of making myself feel better, I usually felt a lot
worse. My misguided attempts to avoid feeling any pain held me
back from doing the healing work I needed to move on with my
life. Sure, it might feel good at the moment to go out and drink
the pain away or send a late-night "I miss you," text, but you'll
always wake up the next morning with the same sadness (and a
really bad hangover).

Instead, there are ways to make a breakup hurt a little less,
and they involve taking care of yourself while you move through
your heartbreak.

UNFOLLOW YOUR EX ON ALL SOCIAL MEDIA

The best favor you can do for yourself is removing every reminder
of your ex from your social media. There's nothing worse than
feeling like you're about to move on from a relationship and then
seeing your ex's face pop up on your Instagram feed. That's a surefire way to start dreaming about everything you miss about them.

I'm not saying you can never check up on your ex again, but for
now, erase their presence from your life. This will give you a fighting
chance to work through your feelings at your own pace; you can
always follow them in the future, once they're a distant memory.

TALK TO ONE OF YOUR FRIENDS EVERY DAY

It's a sad but common truth that people lose contact with their
friends when they get into relationships. I thank my lucky stars
that I have a few solid friends who stuck around in my life, even
when I went radio silent once I got into a relationship. But I can't

say the same for all my friends throughout the years. And I only have myself to blame.

By talking to at least one friend a day, you have a chance to reconnect with people you might've lost touch with since your relationship. Plus, catching up with friends strengthens your platonic intimacy. Friendships can be drama-free, safe, and fulfilling love we carry all throughout our lives, even when romance comes and goes.

CREATE A BREAKUP LIST

Nothing helps me get through a breakup more than a breakup list. Essentially, you want to write down everything you didn't like about your ex or your relationship. Don't skip on even the smallest of details; from how much you hated their beard to the way she talked badly about her friends. Create the list in your phone so it's with you no matter where you go.

Any time you start to feel like you're missing your ex, pull out the list and read it to remind yourself why it's better to keep moving forward without them. When we reflect on relationships in the midst of a major change, we tend to overlook the bad and focus on the good. A breakup list will be your best tool to not fall into thinking your ex is better than they were.

INVEST THE TIME YOU PUT IN THE RELATIONSHIP INTO AN ACTIVITY YOU LOVE

After a breakup, you'll find your days freed up since you're no longer spending time with your ex-boo. Why not use that time to do something you genuinely enjoy?

Whatever activity you choose, do it purely for the sake of how much you enjoy it. Whether that be painting or learning guitar, your activity needs to have no ulterior motive—like getting in shape or advancing your career. It's a sweet little reminder that you deserve happiness. Your emotional state will improve, and you'll be proud of everything new you accomplish.

INDULGE IN SELF-CARE THAT YOU WISH YOUR EX WOULD'VE DONE FOR YOU

If you were the kind of person who waited for your partner to surprise you with a fancy dinner or massage, figure out how to do the same for yourself. If you want a massage, look up your nearest salon and treat yourself (as long as it doesn't break the bank). On your way back home, pick up flowers at your local market. Order a pizza that night and enjoy every slice without worrying about having to share.

By choosing something you wouldn't normally do for yourself, you're creating the subconscious belief you're worthy of these things, regardless of how another person sees you.

GO FOR A WALK AND LISTEN TO YOUR FAVORITE MUSIC

By getting out of your home, you're giving yourself a moment of fresh air and new scenery. It's a chance to breathe deeply and clear your mind of any breakup thoughts. Plus, moving your body releases serotonin, which is a hormone that makes you feel better. I love to go for walks when I'm feeling down; it gets my blood pumping and mind in a better place.

Moving your body will not only make you feel better, but it will also give your mind something to focus on, too. If you're a music or audiobook kind of person, you can listen to them as you stroll through your neighborhood, enjoying the day.

WRITE YOUR FEELINGS INTO EXISTENCE

Keeping your emotions bottled up can make them feel like a dirty secret that has complete control over your life. The moment I told someone how unhealthy my relationship in college was, it felt like I healed an uneasiness I didn't realize was there. I know talking about your feelings can seem scary, so, if that's the case for you, give journaling a shot.

I've been writing in secret since I was young. I'd pour my thoughts out onto a blank piece of paper. I didn't hold back, often writing nonsense simply so I could get the words out. As I got older, I moved those words to the computer and the things I wrote became what launched my writing career.

Of course, you don't have to make your words public. But the power of putting your thoughts onto paper is strong and releases the grip your feelings have on your life.

RE-BUILDING YOUR SELF-IDENTITY

||||||||||

"Life is a journey of winding paths and unknown mountains. sometimes we lose ourselves along the way. it's an act of self-care when you take a detour to find yourself again."

When a relationship ends, it's a disorienting feeling, especially if you're like me; someone who jumps feet first into their relationships. As I said, I'd start imagining my future wedding with someone before we even made it to the third date. I'd get attached to people easily: maybe because I focused too much on my date's great characteristics. But most likely because I hated when I got to know someone and then they'd leave my life. If this sounds like you, a breakup might feel like you aren't sure of who you are anymore.

I once dated a guy named Brandon who was my best friend's roommate (here's another piece of advice: don't date your best friend's roommate). I figured having my best friend and boyfriend in one place would not only be fun but very convenient. Brandon and I constantly hung out together at their Venice house; my best friend and I became enmeshed in his friend group. I went to Phantogram concerts with Brandon and his best friends. I helped throw elaborately themed parties that were Brandon's specialty. I even spent a weekend in Joshua Tree, making s'mores and taking pictures with his friend group.

During those months of my life, I did everything Brandon loved to do. I didn't hesitate to throw myself into his world and let his life consume mine. I stopped doing the things I loved. I dropped essentially all of my hobbies. Seeing friends outside of my best friend became a thing of the past. I barely ever asked Brandon to do things I enjoyed. Even on the one occasion I invited him to an art gallery a drawing of mine was featured in, it felt awkward and like I forced him to be there.

While I don't want it to come off like taking on your partner's interests is bad, losing your identity in a relationship isn't healthy for you in the long run. I thought I could be happy through Brandon's life, but it left me feeling empty—even more so when we broke up. I had a hard time putting the pieces back together when I forgot what they even looked like.

Does this experience feel familiar to you? Perhaps you took on running because your ex ran six miles every morning. Maybe you aren't sure who your friends are anymore because you hung out with their friend group so often. Whatever the changes were that you experienced from your relationship, they expanded your identity. Even if those changes were a result of your partner, they became new parts of your present life. And that might mean you replaced parts of who you were along the way.

After my breakup with Brandon, and neglecting parts of my life, I was stuck thinking, *who even am I?* The mere thought of doing certain things made me nauseous: when someone would mention Joshua Tree or hiking, I'd have uneasy flashbacks of our weekend there.

You may feel lost in a world that keeps moving forward, even though your sense of identity has just been shattered. That's why it's important, when you go through a breakup, to take time to rebuild your identity. Not just in hopes of forgetting about the relationship, but to remind yourself of the parts of *you* you lost along the way.

DON'T BLAME YOURSELF

Relationships end all the time, for a variety of different reasons that are beyond anyone's control. I know it's hard to think past the pain you're feeling now, but I promise one day you'll see this turn of events as a good thing; it means new relationships are in store for your future. Refrain from automatically blaming yourself, or even trying to place blame at all. You did the best you could. You opened yourself to someone new who you didn't know wouldn't be in your life for long, and that's a beautiful act of vulnerability.

It's not helpful, nor is it true, to think you somehow messed up your destiny. You did the most you could by being who you are.

REMOVE ANY REMINDER OF THE RELATIONSHIP FROM YOUR LIFE

You can't expect to heal a wound if you keep going to the source that inflicted the pain. Keeping your ex in your life and expecting to rebuild your identity without them don't go hand in hand. While we'd like to believe "staying friends" can work, there's always someone who gets hurt along the way.

Doing something like texting your ex late at night might feel good now, but you're prolonging the point you feel confident enough to move on with your life. Do yourself a favor: delete their number, unfollow them on social media, and give their stuff to one of their friends so you don't have to see them.

Think of this as your chance to start anew (but maybe keep a letter or two tucked FAR away; those are nice to look back on when you're older).

DO THINGS YOU USED TO LOVE

Before I got in my relationship with Brandon—or the four before that—I used to draw a lot. It's something I can do for hours without realizing time is passing. When I was in my relationship with Brandon, I invested my time into what he loved to do. Once I was single, I promised myself I'd get back into drawing, and there hasn't been a moment I regretted that decision.

You might feel silly at first, picking up a pencil or paintbrush or guitar for the first time in months, but you owe it to your old self to reconnect with the activities that bring you joy now that you're not investing time into a relationship.

CREATING GOALS THAT MAKE YOU FEEL PROUD

Having goals creates specific tasks to focus on and, when you accomplish them, a reason to feel proud of yourself.

Several areas of your life you might want to consider creating goals for are:

- **Finances** (saving X amount of money to be able to afford something you want)
- **Hobbies** (learning how to play your favorite song on the guitar)
- **Fitness** (running a mile in under ten minutes)
- **Career** (taking a certification course or working toward a promotion)

Nothing says, "I know and respect the person I am" like accomplishing the goals you've always wanted to in life.

REMIND YOURSELF HOW GREAT YOU ARE OUTSIDE OF A RELATIONSHIP

Your sense of worth is something only you can determine. Even if another person insists you're amazing, if you don't believe it about yourself, you'll never be able to accept their words. You have to do the work to build your self-worth and create a life you love.

A relationship that helps build your sense of value is unstable. A relationship that supports who you already are, regardless of anything you once saw as flaws, is supportive without exceptions.

REMINDERS FOR WHEN YOUR HEARTBREAK HURTS TOO MUCH

||||||||||

"On the nights when you feel like the pain is too much, know that one day you'll think about this pain from a place where you overcame it; from a place where you're whole, happy, and understand why life played out the way it did."

After Sean and I broke up and I moved away to China, I spent many nights missing him. I'd lie awake in bed, scrolling through photos from trips we went on to Canada and Zion (the rare moments when we were incredibly happy). Even though I knew how horrible we were for each other, I couldn't shake the feeling of missing him. My body ached to be held by his again; I missed the feel of his skin against mine. I let my mind wander back to the days when we were still together because the memories alleviated the pain I felt.

There's going to come a time when you're walking down the street, and you'll see something that reminds you of your ex; maybe someone is eating chocolate ice cream from the same shop your ex was obsessed with. The sight of that ice cream cup will make you feel like your stomach turned upside down. Or maybe, late at night, a rush of emotions will sweep through your body out of nowhere. Deep throbs will course through your veins because your heart is missing someone who was once your everything.

I won't sit here and act like these moments won't come because I'm sure they will. Those moments will hurt. They'll make you question so many of your life choices.

Maybe you'll linger in those thoughts as I did. Most likely for a bit too long. You might feel your heartache for someone you can't have anymore.

When these moments come, I want you to remember these things:

YOU ARE LOVEABLE, NO MATTER SOMEONE ELSE'S DECISION

Everyone is inherently worthy of love. Just because your ex chose to stop loving you or failed to do so in a way you needed, doesn't mean you don't deserve to date someone who appreciates everything about you your ex took for granted.

THIS FEELING WILL PASS; EVEN SOONER IF YOU TRY TO LET IT GO

A feeling only stays in our bodies as long as we allow it to. By thinking more and more about your ex, you're holding on to the emotion of missing them. I know it's hard but distract yourself. Watch a TV show, focus on your breathing, or call up a friend. You'll find those thoughts pass much quicker when you don't give them energy.

YOUR LOVE IS INFINITE, AND THE PERSON WHO HOLDS YOUR HEART WILL BE LUCKY TO HAVE IT

As a human being, you are capable of giving so much love. If you're reading this book, you're most likely a deeply loving person. The person who you choose to give your love to should be grateful and reciprocate those feelings. You deserve a love that isn't one-sided.

LIFE PLAYS OUT IN STRANGE WAYS, BUT IT'S FOR THE BETTER

You might not understand why this is happening to you, but every closed door leads to an open one. You might not be able to see where it will take you now, but I promise there is a better future waiting for you.

YOU HAVE SO MUCH LIFE TO LIVE THAT'S FILLED WITH ENDLESS OPPORTUNITIES

Even when heartbreak feels like the end of your world, it's not. You'll live on. You'll make it through this. One day you'll look back on this breakup and realize how minimal of a life event it was. You have so many other parts of your life to look forward to, love is only one aspect of it.

TEXTING THEM WILL ONLY MAKE THINGS HURT WORSE

You might think a late-night text to your ex will help, but you're only going back to the original source of pain. It's better to grieve the relationship and move through your emotions at your own pace than to try to alleviate your hurt by getting in touch with the person who caused it.

YOUR RELATIONSHIP WASN'T PERFECT; NO RELATIONSHIP EVER IS

We tend to romanticize relationships when we reflect on them (I've found this is even more true when lying in bed late at night). You may think your relationship was perfect, but that's your mind playing tricks on you. Every relationship has its faults; you'll need to remind yourself of that when you're missing them the most.

LOVE WILL COME IN ITS OWN TIME

‖‖‖‖‖‖

"Love is elusive; it plays by its own rules. You can't force it to stay just like you can't try to create it where it was never meant to happen. But love is also worth waiting for because it's one of the most intoxicating experiences you'll go through as a human being. Just make sure you wait for the kind of love that brightens your world, not shatters it. Don't become consumed by your quest for matters of the heart that are out of your control."

You can't force someone to stay in love with you; I learned that the hard way through my relationship with Sean. No matter how much I cried or tried to convince him to stay in our relationship, I wasn't able to change Sean's mind about breaking up.

I made the choice to move to China partly because I couldn't bear the thought of living in the same city as Sean and my life in Los Angeles felt broken. I wanted a new beginning; a drastic change of scenery. A rather long plane ride got me there.

When I landed in Chengdu, I was thrown into a world of new: new foods, new culture, new city, new people, an entirely new language and—as if moving to a new continent wasn't enough to distract me—a new rebound relationship.

In Chengdu, it was typical for the foreigners to congregate at a local bar called Rouge on the weekends. Rouge ended up being the first place I visited when I arrived in my new city. My first night there, I met people from all around the world: France, Brazil, Argentina, South Africa, Senegal, and Morocco. Everyone seemed so friendly, so non-judgmental. I felt at ease even though I was totally out of my comfort zone.

One person who caught my attention straight off the bat was a man named Patrick. His wild brown hair and alluring English accent were beyond my ability to resist. Though I wasn't a fan of his oddly patterned board shorts (yes, he wore swim trunks to a bar), his cheeky smirk distracted me. The moment we started talking, I was hooked on everything he said. What can I say? A British accent is my weakness.

"Let me show you around Chengdu, I know of all the best spots," claimed Patrick after we'd talked a bit. Since I was looking for any sort of adventure that distracted me from life back home, I accepted his offer. We made plans to venture around the city later that week.

Patrick picked me up an hour before sunset on the day of our planned excursion. He pulled up to my hostel on his white Vespa—a typical means of transportation in China, unlike America where electric scooters seem to be hated by all. We raced down the streets of Chengdu, weaving in and out of the crowds. Patrick zipped past the modern downtown buildings and drove along a river, passing nearby pagodas lining the street. We ended our tour at a traditional village known for steamed buns and many, many tourists. Just as we reached the end of the village's alleyways, the city started to glow from the setting sun's golden rays. Patrick could see I was shivering from the breeze, and he wrapped an arm around my shoulder to warm me up. When I looked up to thank him, he smiled and kissed me in a way that felt like my body became alive after two years of painful memories.

Patrick and I continued to date after that night, experiencing an on and off relationship—on and off because I just wasn't ready for something serious. After a particularly eventful night where I was sort of a brat and felt it was in my right to flirt with other guys, Patrick said he couldn't play games anymore. He wanted me to be his girlfriend and, if I didn't want that, we should just be friends.

Afraid of being in the city alone and, also really admiring the person Patrick was, I obliged. Our relationship was made official, and quickly, our small community of foreigners knew we were an item (although they'd already assumed we were).

The sticky summer of Chengdu turned into a cool fall and then an unbearable winter. Between the frigid cold air and unrelenting grey skies, I felt an old acquaintance, depression, creep up on me. I struggled with depression on and off since I was in middle school. I probably felt it with Sean in our relationship, but the constant state of anxiety he put me in overshadowed any other issues I was going through.

BUT I KNEW ONE THING: WHENEVER I WENT THROUGH BAD EPISODES OF MY DEPRESSION, I WITHDREW FROM THE PEOPLE AND THINGS I LOVED IN MY LIFE.

I wasn't happy in Chengdu anymore; friends had come and gone, and I began to detest my new city's gloomy winter skies. I felt a strong desire to be happy that wasn't being satiated in China anymore (or past the first month of my arrival). My instinct to solve my internal struggle was to pack up and move; if I wasn't happy there, I thought, maybe I could be happy elsewhere.

I searched online for a couple of weeks for ways I could work and live in a different country. I found a website that lets you search for jobs working for European families. I found a gig in Barcelona, working as a nanny to two teenage girls. I figured the vibrant culture of Spain would shake my depression out of me (oh how it did not). I reached out to the family, interviewed with them, and the next thing I knew, I was booking a ticket to Barcelona. Patrick knew vaguely of my plans and, though he supported me, the fact he didn't want me to leave hung in the air whenever we were together.

When the day came that I packed up my suitcases and headed to the airport, I'll never forget the sadness on Patrick's face. We weren't breaking up, but it did feel like a death sentence to our relationship. The hopeful romantic in me assured Patrick, and myself, that everything would be fine. We said our tear-filled goodbyes and I left on a flight to the country I'd soon call home.

Though I thought I'd end up going back one day to China to be with Patrick, fate intervened, and I haven't been back since. My depression only worsened in Barcelona, and after two months of being there, I booked a flight back home to live with my parents while I got help.

When I first came back to California, I started hearing from friends who were still in Chengdu that they spotted Patrick hanging out with another blonde woman who obviously wasn't me. Feeling threatened, I questioned Patrick about her. "She's a friend of a friend who's visiting," he insisted, "I've been helping show her around the city with everyone else." I believed him. I mean, what other choice did I have? I lived in California. I had no way of knowing if he was telling the truth all the way in China. That is until another friend who lived in Chengdu saw Patrick kissing that same blonde at one of our favorite bars.

My world shattered; not only was I back home, living with my parents in order to get help for my depression, but my boyfriend cheated on me. I felt betrayed and hurt. I laid under the covers of the bed in my parent's guest room. Tears soaked my pillowcase as my mom tried to console me. She felt awful and mad at Patrick for hurting me like this. After a few days passed, though, my mom brought up a point that still echoes inside me to this day.

"Honey," she said with the extreme, bordering on irritating, concern only a mother could exude, "have you ever stopped to consider how much you really loved Patrick? Not that I think him cheating is at all your fault, but when you love someone, you typically don't leave them. If you were so in love with Patrick, why did you leave China?"

As she spoke, I realized how much truth her words held. This time, it wasn't me trying to force someone to stay; I had been the one who chose to leave. If I loved Patrick and thought we had a future together, why did I move to Barcelona so easily?

I couldn't see then what I can clearly see now: our love was never meant to last because I decided our fate when I moved away. I didn't regret leaving and pursuing what made me happy. But the fact was, my nanny job wasn't some grand opportunity I couldn't pass up, and taking it showed how easily I was willing to leave China and Patrick. I wasn't happy: with China, Patrick, or Barcelona. In fact, I wasn't happy anywhere. And that wasn't something love (or, apparently, deep infatuation brought on by a charming British accent) could fix.

Having been through several good and bad relationships since then, I know now that love isn't something you can force on anyone. It will come in its own time. While that can be a hurtful truth sometimes, it's a magical one at other times.

It's beautiful to think we can choose who we love but crushing to realize we can't choose who loves us back. No amount of convincing or bargaining can spur a feeling of love inside another person's heart. You may think you have a connection that can withstand anything, but it won't always be the case that the other person feels the same.

Through trying to make love happen when I wasn't ready, I caused a lot of pain. I hurt Patrick. He went on to hurt me. I'm not placing the blame on myself or him, it's simply fate that we were never meant to work out. I needed to go through the years following our relationship, when I learned to manage my depression and be alone for a bit. I thought I was ready for a new life in China and a new love with Patrick, but it's not that easy to escape from unresolved pain.

PART III

UNDERSTANDING YOURSELF

SIGNS YOU'VE LOST TOUCH WITH WHO YOU ARE

||||||||||

"The idea that a relationship should consume you is mere poetry. Disappearing so someone else can exist in your life is not a relationship to aspire to."

"I'm sorry for hurting you. This wasn't how I saw our relationship ending," were the last words my ex-boyfriend, Patrick said to me before I hung up the phone. I was angry he cheated and, at the same time, relieved we were over. He lived halfway across the world so I could easily move on and focus on why I came back to California: working through a bad episode of my depression.

All of a sudden, I had a lot of free time; I saw a therapist occasionally and found a job as a barista at a local coffee shop. For the rest of my time, I didn't do anything. I found that being alone with my thoughts for too long wasn't a good thing when I was struggling with my mental health. I needed to fill my days with anything that would keep me from spiraling into negative thoughts.

The problem was, I had no idea what made me happy now that I didn't have much going on in my life. For the first time in a very, very long time, I wasn't dating anyone. All my free time was mine.

Everything I'd done for fun up until this point were things I did with Patrick or in Barcelona. I didn't have mountains to climb or children to nanny. So, what did I even like to do?

I hadn't picked up a pencil to draw in five years. I didn't exercise like I did in college, because again, I did that for a boyfriend. Every show I watched now brought up crappy memories of Patrick. I tried to think of things that would make me happy, but I drew a blank.

This made me realize I lost touch with my authentic self (essentially, me minus all the men). I felt disappointed I didn't have a stronger sense of self. I thought back to my past relationships. There was Sean: I'd given up my relaxed, fun-loving identity for this exercise-obsessed, health-food-eating fanatic I knew he'd adore. And with Patrick, I leaned into my make-plans-at-the-last-minute, down-for-anything-as long-as-I-didn't-break-a-bone side. Now you might be thinking, "Eating well and going on adventures? How in the world is that bad?" And you'd be right if it weren't for the fact that those changes meant abandoning parts of me that I did like. Sure, they had some positive impacts, but so would sharing slices of your pizza with everyone around you, until you realize there's none left for you. That might seem like an extreme (and rather cheesy) metaphor but you get the idea.

I built my relationships up in my head to be these exhilarating experiences, and sometimes they were. But placing them as having the highest priority in my life led to the fact that I couldn't maintain my own identity. Since I wasn't comfortable being myself in my relationships, I ended up feeling constantly misunderstood and emotionally unsafe. I'd created my own suffering, since I wanted to feel accepted yet couldn't be my real self.

When I reflect on those relationships today, I realize that I messed with a crucial part of any relationship: the beginning. From the first date and flirty texts sent, the dynamics between two people form. By starting off my relationships acting like some other person I wasn't, they were always bound to fail. Deep down, I wanted to feel accepted by someone—flaws, insecurities, and awkward mannerisms included—but what I ended up doing was hiding those parts away out of the fear I'd be rejected.

It's not easy to admit you're prone to change the way you act based on who you date. Or maybe you don't even realize the ways you're altering yourself; most of us do so unconsciously. Perhaps you've spent a lot of time pleasing the people around you rather than making sure you're happy first. It's become a habit, rather than waking up every day and thinking, "Today I'll hide who I am in favor of people liking me more."

Luckily, any habit (even one you've been doing for years) can be changed once you realize it exists. Here are some ways in which people lose touch with their authentic self through acts of neglecting their needs, changing themselves, and prioritizing others first:

YOUR PARTNER'S NEEDS CAUSE YOU TO SACRIFICE YOUR OWN

You'll do anything for your partner even if it means exhausting yourself or disrespecting your boundaries. You easily lose sight of what you need from your relationship because you're focused on what your partner wants. You don't feel comfortable speaking up when you're unhappy or when something your partner does makes you feel uncomfortable.

YOU FEEL, AT ANY POINT, YOU MIGHT DO SOMETHING WRONG

You worry your relationships may crumble from the smallest thing. This mentality causes you to need reassurance that the relationship is safe, over and over. Saying sorry and asking, "Is everything OK with us?" feels like second nature. Perhaps you obsessively analyze everything your partner says and does, looking for a sign that confirms your fear the relationship is ending.

YOU FORGET ABOUT YOUR GOALS AND PASSIONS

When you're in a relationship, it becomes your sole focus. If you think back to the days when you were single, you realize you've lost sight of the passions and goals you had in life. You feel like part of you is missing but, for some reason, things can't change. You might even worry your goals would interfere with your relationship; that the two can't exist together.

YOU STOP DOING WHAT YOU LOVE AND ONLY DO THINGS YOUR PARTNER ENJOYS

You go all-in on your partner's interests. You learn how to do the hobbies they love and insist on hanging out with their friends. You feign interest in the things you don't particularly care for, like miniature figure painting (true story). Maybe you don't even remember what you loved to do before the relationship. You're rarely the one to make plans outside of dinner dates or the movies.

YOUR SENSE OF WORTH IS BASED ON THE WAY YOUR PARTNER TREATS YOU

You feel the most confident when your partner praises you and the least whenever you're fighting. You ask for compliments often and worry you're not pretty/smart/fun/interesting enough when your partner doesn't give you them. You alter the way you act, speak, and dress because you believe that's the key to making your partner love you more.

CHASING LOVE WILL EXHAUST YOU

||||||||||

"Focus on the ones who stay. Not the ones you have to convince to stay."

I know all about chasing love. I ended up moving across the globe several times because of it. Don't get me wrong: having a sense of adventure and trying to commit to making a long-distance relationship work are beautiful things. But what I failed to realize was how much I grasped onto the idea a relationship would make me finally feel the happiness I desperately wanted in my life (which said a lot about my self-love).

I cried too many times trying to convince a boyfriend to stay with me. I moved away to a new country when I couldn't convince him. I hoped I'd find this feeling of love I craved: the love my brother never gave me, my dad seldomly showed, and I didn't have for myself. Yet none of those efforts ever worked and I felt utterly exhausted.

It's interesting, looking back, that I chased love like it was a "thing." When you think about it, love isn't physical: it barely has a concrete definition. Love is something you experience, but you have no idea when you'll actually come across it.

Chasing love, when really there's not much to chase, is always going to be an uphill battle. When you want something so desperately, you feel like you're beneath it. When you think a relationship will somehow make you a better person, you're more willing to accept mediocre affection or stay in a relationship that doesn't make you happy.

But our brains don't work that way. You can't imagine what will make you happy until you experience it. Your mind can only think in terms of things you've already experienced; like what happened in your past, who you've dated, and what you've watched in the media. All of that combined creates the idea we have from a young age of what kind of love would fulfill us.

SOMETIMES WE'RE RIGHT ABOUT WHAT WOULD MAKE US HAPPY, BUT OFTEN, WE'RE VERY WRONG.

While I understand why I wanted a relationship so badly—to fill a void I didn't know I had—it seems a bit silly that I pursued it so aggressively. I chased an idea I wasn't even sure was what I wanted. And in return, I felt unworthy of someone's affection and defeated by a concept that's not even physical. Not exactly the best trade-off.

Everyone, including you and me, deserves extraordinary love that surpasses the small idea we created when we were younger about how love should look. Someone who respects and cherishes you. Someone who's not only your partner but your equal. You deserve to stop chasing love. You deserve to have love come naturally, when it's meant to happen.

USE YOUR ENERGY TO CREATE MORE LOVE IN YOUR LIFE

Enjoy your life by doing the things you love most: spending time with the people closest to you, reading books for the sake of entertainment, and drinking coffee that's worth every sip. Love the way the wind makes the trees dance on a cool afternoon. Love the way the warm evening light rests upon the grass as the sun begins to set. Love the big things but, more importantly, the little things.

BE THE LOVER YOU ALWAYS WANTED

Indulge in things that excite your senses and explore the intricacies of your mind. Start journaling. Take yourself on dates. Splurge on your favorite meal. Spend a little extra so you can enjoy your favorite chocolates. Buy *yourself* the damn flowers. Don't wait around for someone else to give you what you can give yourself.

CHALLENGE YOURSELF IN WAYS THAT HELP YOU GROW

And take care of your needs along the way. Celebrate every accomplishment you achieve, even the small ones (I cannot emphasize enough that you need to enjoy the small wins). Whisper kind words to yourself whenever you come across your reflection in the mirror. Learn every little thing about who you are as a unique person on this planet; what clothes feel best on your body, which foods ignite your taste buds, and what you value most in life.

CREATE

If this world needs more of anything, it's for people to create. Whatever it is you love to do—painting, music, writing, cooking—do those instead of worrying over unreturned texts or mixed signals from someone who doesn't reciprocate your affection. I'm sure if you were honest with yourself, you'd say you're exhausted from trying to chase the idea of love. It's like baking homemade cookies: you have better things to do with your Sunday afternoon than chase someone for their cookies, especially when you can make your own and feel proud when they're done.

GETTING IN TOUCH WITH YOUR AUTHENTIC SELF

||||||||||

"Strive to do things with very little regard for what other people will think. Because, if they do think, they'll only do so for a moment. But living out of fear of their moment could impact you for a lifetime."

Understanding who you are outside of a relationship will be the best gift you ever give yourself. No one can take away your identity. It's something that's unique to you and only you. Your authentic self consists of all the little bits that make you a person worthy of happiness, even when you feel like you aren't.

But poor relationships over the years may have buried who you are under layers of insecurities, false beliefs, and criticism. You might feel that, in this exact moment, you can't remember who you were before other people hurt you, which may be as far back as your childhood. But I'm here to say, your true self is still deep inside you, and it's most likely evolved over the years. Only you can uncover and bring those parts of yourself back to light. Sure, you may have collected a few scars along the way that are also part of who you are today, but don't worry; there's not a single person in this world who doesn't have several scars of their own.

When I put my personal life on pause and began understanding why I was so unhappy, I started uncovering parts of myself I forgot about. For instance, I'd always loved deeply, not just for romantic partners, but for my family, friends, the house plants I care for, and animals as well. My fear of having that tender love be rejected drove many of my decisions as an adult. I valued people who were kind and loving but I had no idea how to create a boundary so people who were cruel and unloving didn't come into my life.

You may think the idea of your authentic self is silly, that who you are is who you are. There are even times that are impossible to be your "real self" because social norms just wouldn't be OK with you showing up for a job interview in sweatpants. But any moment you cringe at the way you act, bite your tongue from speaking up, feel misunderstood, or feel the need to be "perfect" are moments that don't have to exist. By accepting your quirks, working on not always pleasing people, and figuring out what brings you joy, you can live a life that feels more "right."

Whether you're currently in a relationship, single, or doing the dance of "it's complicated," the present is always going to be the best time to get in touch with your authentic self. Let's get digging.

START WITH IMAGINING BACK TO WHO YOU WERE AS A CHILD

What were your favorite ways to spend your time? What did you want to be when you grew up? What were some of your favorite memories? What qualities do you think back on and admire most about your younger self? Asking these kinds of questions may seem silly because they're drawing from memories of your past, but who you are today is a collection of all your parts, past experiences included. You'd be surprised what you can learn by reflecting on your childhood. Consider if these past interests, hobbies, memories, and dreams hold any truth to who you are today.

NOW THINK ABOUT WHAT THINGS YOU DO TODAY, OR IN THE NEAR PAST, THAT LIGHT YOUR FIRE

There's a psychological term that I love to use when helping people understand what their biggest interests are. It's called flow: a phenomenon of being so wrapped up in an activity that you completely forget the passage of time. For me, drawing puts me into flow. Give me a pencil and paper and I'll draw for hours without realizing it.

Now I want you to think about an activity that puts you in a flow state. You may have to think back to college, high school, maybe even middle school. Consider what activity puts you in a state where you forget about time to help you determine what hobbies interest you the most. Someone who's in touch with their authentic self knows exactly what activities capture their full attention.

IT'S IMPORTANT TO WRITE DOWN YOUR MORALS AND VALUES

Which qualities about yourself are you proud of? What are characteristics in past romantic partners or friends that made you feel uncomfortable? What statements or topics make your skin crawl or cause you to unfollow people who post about them? If you had the free time, which causes would you volunteer for? All of these are questions to help guide you into understanding what your values are in life. The causes that get you the most worked up are the ones that matter a lot to you. Qualities in past lovers that didn't sit well with you did so because they didn't align with your morals. There's nothing wrong with being religious or completely avoiding spirituality. There's no fault in being a homebody or going out partying every weekend. It's important you understand that these choices are your values, and you want people in your life who respect them. Because there will always be a person who comes along and tries to tear you down according to your beliefs but when you fully understand what they are, you'll feel more confident to walk away from people who don't respect them.

ONCE YOU BEGIN UNDERSTANDING YOUR VALUES, THINK ABOUT YOUR FEARS

What holds you back most from living out your dreams? Is it fear people will judge you? You'll fail? You'll leave this world having never made an impact? If you're honest with yourself, you can narrow your inability to make big life changes or hold firm boundaries down to a couple of main fears. What are those for you? And my next question is, who would you be if you weren't afraid? How would your life look differently if your fears vanished?

KEEP A JOURNAL OF EVERYTHING YOU DISCOVER

Write down your answers to all these questions and any other thoughts that came up for you. You can use this journal to also keep track of your thoughts that pop up throughout the day. Jot down how you feel in certain situations—-powerless? Confident? Unsure? What experiences leave a mark in your memory, what activities or experiences made you feel happiest throughout your day? Writing thoughts down can help you make better sense of complex thoughts. Often, our thoughts get jumbled in our heads or we forget them as quickly as they come. By writing them down, you ensure you won't forget them, and slowly uncover your authentic self that's buried in your subconscious.

START LIVING YOUR LIFE IN A WAY THAT MATCHES THE AUTHENTIC SELF YOU'VE UNCOVERED

After going through all these questions, you'll hopefully have a better understanding of who you were before love hurt you. The things that interested you as a child? Start investing time into those activities again. See if you still have that keen interest in music, painting, building, singing, etc. Your beliefs that people should treat each other with kindness? Only allow people into your life who operate in the same caring manner. Explore the world in a way that respects your authentic self, rather than burying it. Continue to write your experiences down until your authentic self has become your automatic way of existing in this world.

WHAT ARE BOUNDARIES AND HOW TO CREATE THEM

||||||||||

"A home is not meant to keep you hidden away from the outside world. A home is meant to protect you when storms blow and cold nights come. A home is a place where you decide who comes in and when people leave. A home isn't to cut you off from living life; a home is meant to keep you safe."

I've mentioned boundaries a couple of times in this book so far and you may be wondering, what the heck even are boundaries? That's a very fair question. I was in your same shoes at one point, too.

I'd love to say I learned about boundaries when I took a pause from traveling and was living back in California. I'd heard of them but didn't realize how boundaries (or lack of boundaries, I should say) played such a large role in my personal life until I read a book called *Codependent No More*.

It wasn't until a few years later, when I made the conscious decision to stay single for a year, that I started to feel guilt for how my love life played out thus far. I thought: Why did I let so many guys treat me badly? Why did I think it was normal for a boyfriend to have little to no respect for their girlfriend? Why didn't I end the relationships then and there, when my boyfriends acted like complete assholes?

While my guilt didn't help anything (and if you're feeling the same, remember your past exists to teach you lessons), it did get me thinking about why I made decisions that weren't in line with my emotional well-being.

After doing a bit of digging with friends, through books, and a therapy session, the answer became clear: I had zero boundaries. I mean, I probably had some. Like I won't willingly jump out of a plane and I'd rather drink hot sauce than take a shot of tequila. But if you don't already know what boundaries are or weren't taught to create them growing up, you wouldn't naturally have ones that help you create healthy relationships.

When I first stumbled upon the world of boundaries, everything became so clear. A lack of boundaries is the root cause of a lot of people's problems in life, romantic or not. So what are they?

Imagine you're at your favorite beach. You're standing in the middle of a vast open space of sand. You have a stick in one hand, and you're told to draw lines in the sand that people can't cross. At first, you might think, "well don't those lines keep people away from me?" And you'd be half-right.

Think of the stick as your morals and values, and the lines in the sand as limits for what you're willing to accept from someone. You may draw a line in the sand for anyone who disrespects you, or maybe for how much time you can spend helping a friend.

AS LONG AS YOUR BOUNDARY ISN'T DISRESPECTED, PEOPLE YOU'VE CHOSEN TO BE IN YOUR LIFE CAN CROSS THOSE LINES WHENEVER THEY WANT.

But the moment your boundary isn't respected, you have that person step back behind the line so you can have space to heal—or, if they hurt you enough, you take that person out of your life entirely.

Boundaries aren't meant to keep people out of your life: they're meant to keep you safe. Without boundaries, you're at the mercy of whoever wanders into that proverbial sand around you. Your stick is a mere twig, and it's not exactly easy to fend someone off with something that can easily snap.

Which is how I felt when Sean made comments about my weight and I internalized them instead of stating he couldn't talk to me like that. I felt powerless when bad-intentioned people, not just boyfriends, came into my life, and I recognized they needed to leave. Instead of having lines in the sand, I had nothing.

And that isn't to say boundaries are only needed in bad relationships; they're needed in healthy ones, too. No one knows how you want to be treated until you speak up. Someone won't know if the way they act or how much of your time they take up isn't OK until you say something. This applies to romantic relationships, friendships, family, and acquaintances. Boundaries are a part of any healthy human interaction.

I felt a bit overwhelmed when I first realized I didn't have my own personal boundaries, but the process of creating them ended up being an exercise in understanding myself further. Now the question is, how do you create boundaries?

DEFINE YOUR LIMITS

You'll want to write these down. Your limits are emotional and physical points at which you start to feel uncomfortable, stressed, or unsafe. I've found that reflecting on behaviors I disliked most about my exes and friends to be revealing of what my limits are. For example, I don't knock anyone who smokes, but I felt uncomfortable that Patrick smoked cigarettes and weed every single day. Whatever you identify, write it down on a list.

TAKE NOTE OF SITUATIONS THAT BRING UP NEGATIVE EMOTIONS

Another way of determining your limits is noticing, in the moment, when situations make you feel uncomfortable. If a friend makes fun of the way you dress and it actually hurts your feelings, that's a sign of one of your limits. Don't confuse being "sensitive" with understanding your limits; everyone is different.

DECIDE WHAT YOUR CONSEQUENCES WILL BE

If anything, being firm with my boundaries was what I struggled most with. I didn't have the backbone to implement consequences but, without them, my limits were just thoughts in my head. You'll most likely have different consequences for each boundary. Choose for yourself what the consequences will be for people in your life who cross them. Will that look like taking space from someone? Asserting that your feelings were hurt? Or maybe, if it's a romantic relationship, it means breaking up.

SPEAK UP ABOUT YOUR NEEDS AND BE DIRECT

Once you understand your limits, you know your needs. If someone doesn't listen to you while you talk about the bad day you had, let them know you need them to pay attention because talking about your feelings is important to you. Or maybe the way someone constantly challenges your opinions feels disrespectful, in which case, they won't realize that until you tell them. There's no need to complicate your reasoning or beat around the bush. Short, clear, and direct are your best bets.

BE BRAVE ENOUGH TO TAKE ACTION IF YOUR BOUNDARIES ARE CROSSED

Now that you understand your limits, you're able to speak up about them, and you know what the consequences are for people who cross your boundaries, it's time to put them all into play. Without a doubt, people struggle with this step most. Some people are raised being taught that caring for others is their top priority and to always be selfless. I, for instance, had very little self-esteem and struggled to respect my own boundaries for a while. But boundaries really are key to any relationship, and the more you practice using them, the easier they become.

KNOW THAT YOUR BOUNDARIES AREN'T TRUTHS; THEY'RE MERELY YOUR PREFERENCES

If you mention that the way your boyfriend jokes at other people's expense feels rude, but he says it's how he is and he doesn't want to change, neither of you is wrong. You both have preferences and, sometimes, they don't mesh. If I'd told Patrick that I hated his smoking, but he continued to do it anyway, I'd have to consider if that's a dealbreaker for me. He's not wrong for wanting to smoke, but it was a factor in why we weren't right for each other.

SELF-CARE ACTS THAT WILL CHANGE YOUR LIFE

‖‖‖‖‖‖‖

"Instead of focusing on everything you lack. Focus on everything you have. Everything you can give. Everything you've accomplished. Sometimes, it's our mindset that is the part of us that needs the biggest change."

Deciding to pause living abroad to work on my mental health and messed-up love life made me feel like I was a failure. At the time, I felt dejected and uncertain about what my future would look like since I wasn't working a job or doing much of anything, really. I desperately wanted to be happier, but I had trouble seeing the place I was in as the place I was meant to be when everyone else's grass seemed greener (damn you, Instagram).

But I did the work. Through making sense of the beliefs I had, why they formed, and how they affected my life today, I started figuring out what activities helped soothe me during my toughest bouts of depression. I began doing yoga at a local studio and in my parent's backyard on days I couldn't mentally leave the house. I started writing more of my unfiltered thoughts in journals (many, many journals). I interrogated myself with hard questions about why I felt the way I did—ones that revealed how much I hated the person I was.

At that time, self-care wasn't as hot of a topic as it is now. If someone had asked me what I thought it entailed, I'd have said face masks and baths. I had a "treat myself" mentality around it; people needed self-care when they were burnt out from work or school.

But through testing what made me feel better when I felt my worst, I realized self-care extends beyond putting a bandage on an issue. It's not something you do every now and then to escape your reality. Self-care can be done and should be done. Every. Single. Day.

While face masks are great, the impacts of them are short-lived (maybe dewier skin for the day, if you bought a good one). In reality, choosing the right self-care can have lasting impacts that affect your life for a long time to come. You aren't just making yourself happier in the moment, you're working toward a life that feels better every day.

Sure, some of these self-care acts are hard. You'll have to acknowledge the parts of yourself you've always avoided. You'll need to finally make appointments for everything you've been putting off. You might even have to make the hard decision of removing someone who's been in your life for years.

But the self-care that's life-changing doesn't come easy because good things don't come easy. Change in general is hard but in order to make it, you'll need to feel a little uncomfortable at times. Practicing this kind of self-care will help you better understand yourself, prioritize your needs, and show up to life feeling more confident.

APOLOGIZING LESS FOR THINGS THAT AREN'T YOUR FAULT

When you made a mistake, it's important to acknowledge what you did wrong and apologize if needed. But when you reflexively say sorry for things that don't need an apology (speaking up about your opinions, someone bumping into you), it's as if you're apologizing for your existence in this world. You aren't in charge of making others feel comfortable at your own expense. Move through the world with kindness but also do so with integrity.

GOING TO THE DOCTOR REGULARLY

You'd want a child or your loved one to ensure they're in good health on a regular basis. Why don't you do the same for yourself? Scheduling doctor appointments as needed, rather than putting them off, is an ultimate form of self-care. Trust me when I say, it's better to know than to worry. I put off too many doctor's appointments that simply prolonged healing from old injuries I had. Besides, you can't chase your dreams and show up as your best self when you're not your healthiest self.

BEGIN ASKING FOR WHAT YOU WANT

When you stay silent instead of expressing your needs, you're reaffirming any beliefs you have that you're not worthy of care. Many people do this because they were taught to keep the peace or not be a burden to others. But it's about time you let that shit go. Your needs matter just as much as anyone else's. You deserve to ask for them as much as anyone else. When you feel yourself shying away, become clear on what you want to ask for. Tell yourself, "I deserve to have my needs met," and speak aloud with confidence. You might feel overwhelmed at first, but the more you practice stating what you need, the easier it becomes.

LETTING GO OF FRIENDSHIPS THAT DRAIN YOU RATHER THAN LIFT YOU

One of the hardest things to do in life is be honest with yourself about if a friendship has run its course. By allowing people who drain you to stay in your life, you're letting them drag you down and use up your precious energy. Your happiness is a sum of the way you spend your time. Some friendships aren't meant to last forever, and you're better off removing the ones who hold you back from being the person you want to be.

LEARNING HOW TO ENJOY SOLITUDE

When you come home at night to an empty apartment, how you feel at that moment says a lot about how much you enjoy your own company. There's a choice to feel lonely (a negative emotion) or solitude (a positive one). You can learn how to love spending time alone or avoid it at all costs for the rest of your life. But one thing is for sure: the only person's company you'll always have with you throughout your life is yours. A beautiful act of self-care is learning to enjoy it.

UNFOLLOWING ACCOUNTS ON SOCIAL MEDIA THAT MAKE YOU FEEL BAD ABOUT YOURSELF

Social media is a black hole for self-confidence. When you're constantly bombarded with photoshopped models and picture-perfect couples, it's almost impossible not to compare your life to those images. Besides, most of the time those people are trying to sell you on their "perfect" lifestyle; of course they want you to feel like your life isn't as good as theirs.

But you can't fall into the trap of comparison if those photos aren't in your feed. Unfollow any account that makes you question how much you love your life. A constant reminder of everything you don't have compared to others would tear even the most confident person down.

CREATING BOUNDARIES WITH THE PEOPLE CLOSEST TO YOU

Drawing boundaries with people in your life will make your relationships stronger (refer to the "What are Boundaries and How to Create Them" chapter). I know that seems counterintuitive, but it makes a lot of sense. When you allow someone to take from you, whenever they please, you're letting them have control over your resources (time, energy, happiness). Eventually, you'll begin to resent them. You'll quietly let that relationship turn into one you can't stand.

Instead, create clear boundaries for people so they know how you expect to be treated and what hurts your feelings. They might push back at first, but stand firm. Boundaries are the only way to make sure your needs are respected.

LEAVING A JOB THAT YOU DREAD

You'll spend one-third of your life driving to and being at your job. If you wake up every morning resenting the fact that you have to go to work or you fantasize about calling in sick, it's time to consider looking for a new job. I know that not everyone is in a position to completely change careers. But if you're able to make a plan to do so, or even pivot into a new company that cares about their employees more than your current one, you owe it to yourself and the people in your life to make that change. You spend enough of your life at your job that you deserve to enjoy the work you do.

FINDING A GREAT THERAPIST FOR WHENEVER YOU NEED TO TALK

Your friends and family might suffice as people to vent to, but they're not trained professionals. It can be mentally taxing for a loved one to always be your source for emotional needs. I'd be irresponsible to say that all issues can be fixed with a book or by talking to a friend. Some are much deeper and need to be worked through with a trained professional.

A therapist can help you uncover trauma that happened in your past that's currently affecting your life. They're trained to provide you with exercises to help you work through any painful memories or hard times that you're currently going through. While I'm all for having a support system composed of those closest to you, a therapist will work wonders beyond what your loved ones can do. And most of the time, you can find affordable therapy online or at your nearest community center.

LOVING YOUR LIFE WILL ATTRACT MORE LOVE

‖‖‖‖‖‖‖

"There's something about a person who's living their best life that other people who are doing the same can't help but be attracted to."

Everywhere you turn, someone is talking about how to get love. Articles are written about attracting your dream man or how to win over a woman on the first date. Books explain the secrets of changing your personality so more people like you. The emphasis always seems to be on how to get others to show their affection.

Very few people talk about creating love. How, by doing the things you're passionate about most and showing your appreciation to those closest to you, you'll attract even more love into your life. Better yet, this kind of love won't be the type you have to fight for: it'll be the kind that comes naturally to you. The kind of love you always wished you had.

After I spent time back home with my friends and family, I felt like I was in a better mental space. I made plans to live abroad one last time after I found out I could teach English in South Korea, make enough money to live, save a bit, and see a new country. Why not one last adventure, I thought.

I landed in Daegu, South Korea with an entirely new mindset compared to what I had in China or Spain. I wanted to really experience the Korean culture, but I wanted to do so by respecting my own unique interests. I was lucky enough to land a job teaching conversational English to adults at a school downtown. My students became my friends very quickly, which meant, aside from one Canadian girl who I became friends with while there, all of my friends were locals. This was wildly different than when I lived in China, seeing as I hung out solely with the foreigner community. My students in Daegu introduced me to new traditions, like rolling gimbap in the perfect way so it doesn't fall apart. They taught me about how important friendship is in Korean culture: always helping me with anything I had trouble with, like setting up my phone plan. And they accompanied me while sight-seeing around the country and visiting foreign villages.

Korea was a chapter in my past where I learned how to truly enjoy life itself. I built lasting friendships. I learned how to lean on people when I needed help. I explored new interests, from fostering a cat to finally learning how to cook more than scrambled eggs.

What inadvertently happened was that I began enjoying my day-to-day life in a way I previously held myself back from doing. I created love in my life, and without even trying, attracted an epic romantic love story as a result. But more on that later.

WHEN YOU PURSUE THE KIND OF LIFE YOU GENUINELY ENJOY, YOU BECOME HAPPIER AND ATTRACT THAT KIND OF HAPPINESS ELSEWHERE.

The people who are out in the world, leading a positive life filled with their passions, won't be attracted to others who aren't doing the same. And, on the flip side, when you're unhappy, you're more likely to attract other unhappy people into your life.

It's like when you're having a shitty day. Have you ever noticed that when your morning starts off terrible, it's easy to come across other people having a crappy day, too? It's a weird phenomenon, but like energies attract each other.

Typically, when people realize their life isn't making them as happy as they expected, they do one of two things: mask their unhappiness with external, temporary fixes (relationships, partying, drinking) or change their life to create long-lasting happiness. By doing the former, you're falling into the trap of thinking happiness comes from different external aspects of life. When you commit to a life-long change, you take happiness into your own hands.

Pursuing interests, activities, and people who make you feel full, rather than drain you, radiates loving energy into your life. You start to enjoy the way you spend your downtime. You might realize working eight hours a day at a job you don't like isn't for you. You invest your time into people who care about and cherish your presence. Living a life like this, in turn, makes you someone who people want to be around because you're radiating the love everyone craves more of in their life. One day, without even realizing it, you'll look around and see how your zest for living attracted more love into your life without you even trying.

OVERCOMING YOUR INSECURITIES AND FEELING MORE CONFIDENT IN YOURSELF

||||||||||

"The most important part in all of this is to never give up hope that your life can look wildly different than it does now. That you're capable of the happiness that exists when your mind wanders to a life where you were never told that you didn't deserve all that you want in life."

Insecurities are nasty. They can keep you from creating the changes you desire most and leave you stuck in a relationship that doesn't make you happy. But until you confront your insecurities, understand where they came from, and work on getting rid of them, they'll hold you back from moving through life confidently.

Once I was settled and living in South Korea, I got a familiar urge to download Bumble and see what kind of guys were looking to date in Daegu. I found a lot of local men, and, to my surprise, many American men from the local Naval base. But one guy who stood out was a tall, blonde, French guy whose profile picture was him posing with the Ninja Turtles in Time Square.

I swiped right and we matched. His name was Alexandre, Alex for short. Turns out, he moved to South Korea for an internship as part of his master's program. We went on our first date to a famous bibimbap restaurant in downtown Daegu. Again, I'm a sucker for accents, and Alex's French pronunciation of English words was alluring. That and the fact he was funny, kind, and excited to finally meet someone who wasn't Korean.

Alex and I went on a second date to a local, rural village where we explored the pagodas and talked about our respective lives back home. When the sun began to set, we shared our first kiss next to a small lake illuminated by warm string lights. It was magical.

We continued dating and became official a few months in, but I always knew Alex would have to leave Korea before I did. His internship ended after I'd been there for three months and he had to go back to France to finish his program. When that time came, we had the not-so-fun talk about what that meant for our relationship.

To my surprise, Alex offered me something wild. "Move to Paris with me," he said. His offer sounded like something I'd only imagine happening in sappy love movies. Instead of jumping at the idea, I took a few days to think. I didn't want to leave my teaching job and burn the bridge with the people at my school. They'd given me a great opportunity and I had nothing but positive experiences because of that school.

After considering everything that was going on in my life, I told Alex I'd move to Paris with him after I finished a few more months of teaching. We did long-distance for a bit, which wasn't as hard as I thought it would be, and two months later, I boarded a plane for Paris.

It sounds like every person's dream, right? To live in Paris with their partner and explore a new country? I thought the same, but

I ended up being a bit too hopeful about my new move. At first, Paris was great. I was able to find a remote marketing position to pay the bills. I studied French in high school and college, so I was able to practice the language more. Our apartment was beautifully quaint (though it had no elevator and we lived on the seventh floor).

But being in a new city, where I worked from home and Alex worked at an office, quickly made me feel lonely. It was hard to make friends in the city of love, and I began resenting how much I relied on Alex for companionship.

When you share that much of your time with someone and they're your only source of intimacy (platonic or not), issues begin popping up that were never there before. Alex was a funny, young guy who exuded romance. But whenever we fought, I felt my fear of abandonment creep up on me. When he would talk with his girl friends in French, I'd wonder what they were saying; my mind would race to thoughts of him dating someone who was prettier, more fun, or smarter than I was.

When the time came that I had to move back to the United States because of visa restrictions, and Alex and I promised to "figure out a plan to live together again," my worries amplified. Every argument felt like it would be the end of us; every time he went out with friends, I'd fear he would change his mind.

All of those worries and self-criticisms I had were my insecurities. My relationship with Alex was just one example of how they affected my love life, but my insecurities caused harm in a lot of other places besides my dating life.

In short, insecurity is when you lack confidence in a certain aspect of your life. Maybe you don't feel confident about your looks, or perhaps your ability to do your job. Maybe you feel like your life is a mess or that you're a failure. Or, maybe you're like I was, and you don't feel good enough for love. Whatever your insecurities may be, you probably feel like they hold you back from living your life fully.

But the good news is, you don't have to feel like a victim to your insecurities forever. How would I know? I worked through a lot of mine. Sure, they pop up every now and then, but being aware of their existence and working to change their power over me helped me overcome a lot of the ways they held me back.

IT'S IMPORTANT TO KNOW THAT YOUR INSECURITIES AREN'T YOUR FAULT

Most of the time, our childhood and experiences while growing up affect who we are as adults. If your parents were the kind of people who constantly criticized you for being slow, you'll feel triggered when someone calls you dumb or makes fun of the way you talk.

The same concept even applies to experiences you had later in life, too. If an old boss called you dumb over and over at your job, you could carry that belief with you for the rest of your life. Traumatic experiences might be something obvious, but they can also be seemingly insignificant scenarios that left a lasting impression. While you're in no way at fault for the insecurities you have as an adult, you're the only person who can make the decision to work on them.

GET TO KNOW YOUR INNER VOICE AND WHAT IT SAYS

Every person has what's known as an "inner voice." It's the voice you hear when you do things like think or read a book. But it's also the voice inside some people's heads that criticizes them for the things they do throughout the day. While the inner voice may seem like it would have little impact on you since it's not physical, it actually does a lot of mental damage, especially when left unchecked.

Think about it: would you want to be friends with someone who constantly called you stupid? That whenever you did something wrong like forgot your keys or dropped your phone, called you thoughtless? Chances are, you'd listen a few times before you stopped hanging out with them altogether. Well, your inner voice is no different.

When you constantly hear criticizing remarks about the person you are, you'll begin internalizing those messages and believe there's something wrong with you. Then your actions change based on those beliefs, all because of the voice in your head; the voice that is wholly wrong and driven by your insecurities.

The greatest change I made for my insecurities was recognizing the words my inner voice said. If I made a mistake at work, I'd call myself dumb. If Alex and I got in a fight, I'd call myself worthless. Just by taking note of what I told myself, I created an opportunity for me to change what my inner voice said. Because while those thoughts came without us even trying, we have the ability to halt them in their tracks.

ASK YOURSELF WHERE THESE BELIEFS COME FROM

When you call yourself dumb, dig deep to figure out when that belief formed. Chances are, it didn't just come out of nowhere. Did your mother often call you careless? Or maybe an ex-boyfriend? While it's not crucial to understand where your ideas about yourself stem from, it's a great step towards realizing how little truth they hold.

When you understand why your false beliefs about yourself formed, you can find reasons to affirm opposite beliefs. You won't be so quick to think you're worthless if you picked up that thought from your crappy ex-boyfriend with his own insecurities. Instead, you can think about all your strengths and quickly realize you're in no way worthless.

ACT IN WAYS THAT DEFY YOUR INSECURITIES

You've pinpointed your insecurities, recognized when you say them to yourself, and understand why they exist. Now comes the hard part of changing your beliefs and habits.

The first part of overcoming your insecurities is changing what your inner voice says. Whenever I noticed that I called myself stupid, I'd replace that thought with words of affirmation like, "you make mistakes, just like everyone else, but that doesn't mean you're a bad person." Or even something simple like, "you're fat" into "your body is beautiful."

The second part is to not let your insecurities dictate your life. If you want to wear a shirt but worry about what people will think about how tight it is, wear the shirt anyway. When you think you'll mess up a presentation at work, walk into the meeting believing you already nailed it. The only way to overcome your insecurities is to replace and defy them. And trust me when I say that living a life where you're not held back from false beliefs you picked up in life begins creating confidence that you have more control than you think.

INCREASES YOUR CONFIDENCE THROUGH LIFE CHOICES

Once you begin doing the work to overcome your insecurities, you don't want to fall back on old habits that will keep you stuck and feeling unconfident. There are a few changes to your life that you can make, to not only increase your self-esteem but help make sure those old insecurities stay in the past where they belong.

DON'T HANG OUT WITH PEOPLE WHO MAKE YOU FEEL BAD

Letting go of friendships can be one of the hardest things to do. When you've known someone for a long time, you might feel obligated to keep them in your life. But the reality is, not everyone is meant to be in your life forever. People come and go. You need to look out for your mental health first.

A great rule of thumb that helps me determine if a friend is someone who I want to keep in my life is asking myself if I feel bad about myself after we spend time together or fulfilled. I had to make the difficult decision to end a college friendship of three years. We'd been best friends, but I'd grown out of our petty gossip and toxic dynamic. I miss her from time to time, but I know we're better off on separate paths.

STOP FOLLOWING ACCOUNTS ON SOCIAL MEDIA THAT TRIGGER YOU

I'm not just talking about the bikini models on Instagram who make you feel like your body isn't beautiful. Unfollow any account that triggers you or makes you feel like your life lacks everything they have.

It was hard to come to terms with the fact that I don't need a good reason to unfollow someone. They could post the most positive content, but if I feel worse after watching their stories or like an insecurity of mine is being poked, I unfollow them. I now treasure my mental security and that will always come before someone's social media account.

NOTICE YOUR BODY LANGUAGE

People tend to make themselves smaller when they don't feel confident. It's a way of protecting themselves from any emotional harm they're scared might happen.

But studies have shown that having an open, inviting body posture increases a person's confidence. Standing tall, with your shoulders back and a smile on your face will make you feel like you're more in control of situations. Of course, do what feels natural but be aware that we often use body language as a way for our insecurities to be expressed.

STOP COMPARING YOURSELF TO OTHERS

And I mean anyone. Your colleague. Friends. Family. That woman you see on TikTok.

When you place your value on the act of comparing yourself to other people, you'll always feel like you're not enough. Even the most confident person will find someone who has more than them.

Comparison isn't a good marker for how well you're doing in life. Most people only publicly display the parts of their life they're proud of. They don't talk about all the failure, difficult emotions, arguments, and uncertainty they experience.

Everyone comes from different life circumstances. Everyone has their struggles. Everyone has their own insecurities. But you'll never be able to know all of that. Your best bet in life is to focus on your own lane and where you're going, rather than looking around and seeing what everyone else is doing.

BE YOUR BIGGEST FAN

The best way to increase your confidence is to be your biggest fan. If you wait around for everyone else to be happy for you to the extent you want them to be, you'll be sorely disappointed.

Instead, be the one who celebrates all your wins, whether they're big or small. Cheer yourself on and give yourself pep talks when you need them. Believe in yourself more than you've ever believed in anyone.

You can still rely on your support system, but know you can accomplish whatever you set your mind to and you're deserving of happiness in your life. If you can accomplish this, you'll be set for a life where your emotions feel valid, your dreams supported, and you feel like you can take on the hard times when your confidence falters.

WHY TAKING A BREAK FROM DATING COULD BE EXACTLY WHAT YOU NEED

||||||||||||

"Vulnerability starts with being vulnerable with yourself. How can you step into a life of courage if you're afraid to acknowledge all of you? The memories that hurt, the parts you're not proud of, your faults, your insecurities. Until you're able to look in the mirror and confront everything, you won't be able to experience true vulnerability with others."

If you're like me, you feel pressured to constantly be searching for that special someone. The idea of ever slowing down when it comes to dating isn't part of the narrative you've been told. There's always someone in your life—whether it be your parents, grandma, or nosey neighbor—who pressures you to stay on this imaginary love timeline of being married by twenty-six and having kids by twenty-eight. Even movies depict marriage as something someone should search for until it's finally obtained.

I always thought, "If finding a partner is an end goal in life, who has time for a pause?" (just typing that felt a bit nauseating).

But this old-school way of thinking does all sorts of harm to your psyche. If you believe something is essential to the complete-ness of your life, you become consumed by the journey. So much so, that you lose a little (or a lot) of who you are along the way. Dating and finding a life partner can be a lot of fun. But if you're finding yourself in one unhealthy relationship after the next, or continually feeling drained by the process of dating, maybe what you need isn't more dates. Maybe what you need is a break.

Taking a pause from dating was one of the best decisions I made for myself, even though it wasn't an easy choice. I was what many call a "serial monogamist." My first relationship started when I was fifteen and barely knew anything about boys. But even though that was the case, I still carried on having boyfriend after boyfriend for the decade after that. Even when I moved back from living in South Korea and France and stopped dating Alex after a year (we couldn't find jobs in the same country), I dated two more men who ended up topping my list of most unhealthy relationships. I'm not knocking monogamy; I'm a fan of it. But I spent over ten years of my life coupled up. I wish I would've slowed down and stayed single for a bit of that time.

After those two unhealthy relationships, I finally decided enough was enough. I needed to take a break from dating. I want-ed to explore who I was, what my beliefs were, and what I wanted out of life, but I needed to figure all of this out when I wasn't in a relationship. While I think it's possible for someone to do this kind of work when they're with a partner, doing it while you're single will be easier.

I made a pact to myself that, for one year, I wouldn't get into a serious relationship. I wanted to use the year to finally step back from my love life and just enjoy being single. I could make choic-es for myself, without another person influencing my decisions. I was able to finally spend all my time with just me, myself, and I; exploring what life had to offer with no concern for someone else's opinions.

I realized all those dating pressures we experience are a lie; there's so much value to be had in pressing pause on the dating process. If you're just getting out of yet another relationship or feeling fed up from dating, a break could do you wonders, too. You don't have to take off a year as I did, but even a few months could shake things up in the best way for you. Here's why:

IT'S A CHANCE TO REFRESH

If you do anything for too long, dating included, it will start to get stale. Worse, you may even become stuck in patterns you don't realize aren't serving you anymore. Taking a step back from dating allows you to breathe, relax, and refocus your energy on another part of your life for a bit.

YOU AREN'T CONFRONTING THE PARTS OF YOU THAT ARE IN PAIN

Instead, you're diverting your attention to relationships that distract you at the moment but leave you feeling empty. Whenever a relationship ends or someone ghosts you, you'll be back at square one. No amount of dating will keep you from eventually having to face the pain that's controlling your life.

YOU AREN'T CLEAR ON YOUR BOUNDARIES AND BECAUSE OF THIS, YOU FIND YOURSELF WONDERING WHY YOUR RELATIONSHIPS DON'T LAST LONG OR WHY OTHERS HURT YOU

The people you date will never meet your expectations because they don't know what those expectations are or you're not willing to leave if they're not met. You're more often left feeling exhausted because having your boundaries crossed time and time again feels like a personal violation.

YOU AREN'T IN TOUCH WITH WHO YOU ARE OUTSIDE OF A RELATIONSHIP

You've been in relationships for the majority of your life to the point that you don't feel whole outside of them. Whenever a breakup happens, it feels like you lost part of your identity. But the truth is, you're not a half waiting for another half. You're whole outside of your relationships. You're just buying into a false narrative that tells you you're lacking.

YOU'VE BECOME CYNICAL ABOUT DATING

Since you've had plenty of bad dating experiences, you've fallen into the trap of thinking all of dating is hopeless. That kind of attitude breeds negativity and the people you date can pick up on that energy. Continuing to try and find someone who will surprise you isn't the fix; your mindset is. Your thoughts are more powerful than you think.

DATING IS HOLDING YOU BACK FROM PURSUING YOUR GOALS

You seem to make big life decisions based on the person you're dating at the time. You believe sacrificing your needs for your relationships is how love works, instead of realizing compromise is a two-way street. Now that another relationship ended, you wonder why you let someone else sway your decisions about major goals.

YOU NEED TO RE-CONNECT WITH OTHERS IN YOUR LIFE

You've lost touch with family. You barely remember the last time you hung out with your friends in-person. You were so consumed by dating, you let your other relationships fall to the wayside rather than incorporating them into your life. You miss those people when you think about them and wish you could change things back to the way they were.

THE THINGS THAT HAPPEN WHEN YOU TAKE A ONE-YEAR BREAK FROM DATING

⠀⠀⠀⠀⠀⠀⠀⠀⠀⠀

"We live in a world where we're taught to go go go. But humans are soft; we have feelings and limits. That doesn't mean we are somehow wrong. It means the system we live in is wrong. It means there's value in resting; in taking pauses. But we have to be the ones to prioritize that for ourselves in a world that tells us to do the opposite."

I sat in my room, tears rolling down my cheeks. Mere minutes before, I'd watched another relationship end, this time, on my own front porch. It wasn't a breakup you'd see in a movie like *The Notebook*. It wasn't much of anything, really. After what seemed like our hundredth fight, he finally suggested we break up. I sighed with relief and told him I agreed. Both of us knew the relationship would never go anywhere; we had a very common case of never being on quite the same page. In all honesty, I wanted something more serious and he just wanted to have fun. I didn't blame him. So why, then, did I feel heartbroken by yet another man I didn't care too much about?

My reaction to the breakup came like a reflex. I wiped the tears from my face and reached for my phone on my bedside table. I re-downloaded my go-to dating app, updated my profile, and began swiping. I'd swiped left on about ten profiles before it even hit me. Why was I trying to cover up my sadness from this failed relationship by jumping into more dating? What would stop me from making the same mistakes I'd always made?

Luckily, I have my best friend, Dannie, who helped me as much as he could through a relationship that was obviously destined to fail. Each time my then-boyfriend and I got into a fight over the most ridiculous things, I explained all the details to Dannie, and, like a great best friend would, he helped me understand my feelings towards the situation rather than talk crap.

When the breakup inevitably happened, Dannie helped me get to a point where I started questioning why I acted the way I did in relationships. And rather than wallow, I did some research.

I read countless articles and books about love and adult relationships. If you haven't read them already, *Attached*, *The Five Love Languages*, *Essays in Love*, and *Codependent No More* are eye-opening books. They put all the complicated experiences I was going through into words. Those books helped me feel understood and like I wasn't going crazy.

Those books, talking with Dannie about my feelings, and seeing a therapist a couple of times (again, I can't recommend therapy enough, even if it's a free group counseling session) helped me clearly see the themes that ran through my love life. I realized I fell for the age-old trap of dating the same man with different faces and that ultimately, dating made me more unhappy than happy. I brought to light the fact I dated to try and receive validation from other people. I used that feeling to reassure myself I was worthy of people's love in this world.

Once I lifted the veil and started to see my behaviors for what they were, I knew I needed a break from dating.

I promised myself, at that moment, I would stay single for a year. I deleted every dating app on my phone. I put romance on the back burner and focused on other parts of my life. With the free time I had, I finally opened my life up to a few changes it always needed.

I'LL BE HONEST: AT FIRST, BEING ALONE FELT EXTREMELY UNCOMFORTABLE.

I was used to having an emotional support net composed of whoever I was dating at the time. I always experienced my emotions, but I didn't have to sit with them alone. But during this break, on the nights when things were hardest, I didn't have a boyfriend to turn to. It was just me, my feelings, and the truth in them that was slapping me in the face, waiting to be realized. Sure, I could mindlessly scroll through social media to distract myself, but that only got me so far.

I saw being alone as loneliness, rather than solitude. I'd forgotten what I liked to do with my free time; I didn't see my apartment as a retreat, but rather, a prison. It was clear I needed to work on getting to know the parts of me I buried deep inside, covered by the comfort of my relationships.

But the more time that passed and the more realizations I made, being alone didn't feel like a cure but rather, a gift. I wanted to make big changes, and by not being in a relationship, I had a whole lot more free time than I normally did. My nights? All mine. My weekends? I could choose to do what I wanted. And though I didn't know how I wanted to spend that time at first, I started exploring new and old hobbies: drum lessons, learning to craft the perfect pot of coffee, and digging up my old sketch pad from college. I watched every cheesy romance movie I could find on Netflix and volunteered with organizations I loved.

With this newfound free time, I also gained the mental clarity to work on the goals I had for myself. At the same time as my last breakup (which was the relationship before meeting my current beau), I was fired from a technical recruiting job I regretted ever taking. I knew I didn't want to go back to recruiting, but I only had a vague idea of the career change I wanted to make. I'm beyond grateful I was gifted with the time and opportunities to be able to explore options. If I'd gone through this process while in a relationship, I probably would've pulled the classic move of letting my partner's opinions fog my judgment. Being unemployed and taking up a nannying job to make ends meet wasn't exactly something I felt proud about at first, but everything worked out the way it was supposed to in the end. Not only did I end up loving my time nannying, but it provided me time to start my writing career.

As a result of getting more comfortable spending time alone in my apartment, I began to realize I didn't need to be in a relationship. I decided that, when I made the choice to date again, I'd be extra vigilant of any red flags. The moment someone started waving a red flag or disrespected me, I'd be out. I raised my standards for how I expected someone to treat me, and in turn, believed in myself enough to know how much I deserved.

I questioned the narratives I believed about love, the shattering words my exes told me, and how my underlying insecurities only seemed to get worse in relationships. It was clear I had two choices: I could continue to blame other people for my unhappiness or finally decide for myself how my life would turn out.

LITTLE REMINDERS FOR WHEN YOU FORGET YOUR SELF-WORTH

You're bound to have nights when you feel horrible and moments when you're down, uncertain, or confused. Those feelings will disguise themself as indicators there's something wrong with you. When that time comes, don't buy into that lie.

I remember sitting on the floor of my studio in South Korea. Some apartments there have floor heaters where the ground literally warms up the room: the floor is like a giant heating pad. On particularly cold nights, I'd lay on my laminate floors with my foster cat, Jiji, and watch a move on my laptop.

I had the week of Christmas off from work, which I spent alone. I'd just started dating Alex and he went home to see his family in France. All of my friends in Korea were, understandably, with their families for the holidays. I had Jiji, but even she would leave me to go sit on a particularly warm patch of the ground underneath my bed.

So, I opted to watch *The Holiday* that night: my go-to movie for when I feel down. And since I know the movie, almost line for line, my mind started wandering to thoughts of my past.

I was still new to the whole "self-aware" life. I'd pinpointed specific moments where I'd made bad decisions, stumbled along my present self-care journey, and was letting my insecurities run around like vicious toddlers. Being alone on Christmas and having a lot of time to lay on my floor and just think ended up becoming a mountain of loneliness that was hard to overcome.

I thought about Sean and how I wished I stood up to him when I had the chance. I thought about the time I wasted in China while silently struggling with my mental health. I wondered what those choices said about me as a person. I thought about what people must think (and by that, I mean, people on Facebook who I went to high school with), seeing poor me, without a straight path in life; not climbing the corporate ladder or starting a family like people back home. I dipped into a deep sadness that night, feeling like I'd never get to a point where I felt happy or certain of who I was.

But eventually, years later, I did start to change those beliefs. The shift was slow, and I had to remind myself time and time again of how wrong the ideas I had about myself were. But with time and dedication, I changed my self-worth because of a few realizations.

You're bound to stumble, especially when it comes to your self-confidence. When the world holds up a mirror to you through everything you do, it's only natural to question if who you are is good enough. Self-doubt will creep into your life through the smallest cracks, but when it appears, remember these little reminders of how much value you inherently hold:

YOU DETERMINE THE VALUE OF OTHER PEOPLE'S OPINIONS

There will come a time—probably many times—when someone will try to make you feel bad about yourself and question your worth. But at the end of the day, their opinion only holds as much value as you allow it to. You can let their comment define who you are or decide no one's opinion determines your worth but your own.

NO ONE CAN TAKE AWAY FROM YOUR WORTH IN THIS WORLD

You are inherently worthy: of love, of success, of your biggest goals and dreams.

YOU MIGHT NOT KNOW WHAT YOU'RE DOING RIGHT NOW, BUT THAT'S OKAY

You're not wrong if you're not sure what you want in life, especially when people are so quick to pressure you into making decisions. It's a sign of growth to question what makes you happy, if you want more from life, and to be curious about how other choices can lead you there.

NO ONE HAS EVERYTHING FIGURED OUT NOT A SINGLE PERSON IN THIS WORLD KNOWS EXACTLY WHAT THEY'RE DOING

But that's what's fun about life. Something new is always just around the corner; you don't know where your journey will take you but that's most likely because you can't fathom how fulfilled your new path will make you feel.

PEOPLE AREN'T JUDGING YOU LIKE YOU THINK THEY ARE

People are preoccupied with thinking about themselves. If they do think about or judge you, it's only for a moment. Don't let their small moment shape the choices that affect you for a lifetime.

YOU'RE EXACTLY WHERE YOU'RE MEANT TO BE IN LIFE

Where you are right now might be a lot different than how you thought life would turn out, but your present is where you're meant to be. If you want to create change, use all the lessons you've learned up until this point to light the way down a new path.

YOU'LL GET THROUGH THE THING YOU THINK YOU WON'T GET THROUGH

The moments when you feel like your world is over are hard to get through, but they're not the end. You will make it to another day. You won't be forever tormented by the emotions you're experiencing now. You'll make it past this, and you'll be stronger on the other side.

SOMEONE WHO DESERVES TO BE IN YOUR LIFE WILL MAKE TIME FOR YOU

If you need to convince someone to be in your life, then let them go. Someone who doesn't make time for you is making their priorities clear. The people who matter are the ones who want to be in your life.

YOU'LL QUESTION YOUR SELF-WORTH FOR A LONG TIME TO COME

It's an indication of growth; of your refusal to be complacent, of your ability to see how your life could be rather than where you are now. Don't get mad at yourself for falling back into negativity; know it'll happen and come back to the self-work you've done.

PART IV

FINDING A GREAT PARTNER

HOW YOUR DATING PATTERNS ARE HOLDING YOU BACK FROM LOVE

||||||||||||

"Let your reaction to their inaction guide you into understanding more about yourself. Ask why you're willing to invest energy into someone who invests so little of theirs into you. Ask yourself what belief you hold that makes you think you don't deserve better."

Think about the way your dating life has gone so far. Are there any similarities between your past relationships? Do your dates usually fizzle out in the same ways? Do you keep attracting the same kind of person into your life: someone who wouldn't make for a happy relationship?

Pinpointing common themes in your romantic life can help you uncover your dating patterns. Dating patterns are the choices you make and the habits you have surrounding dating and love. Sometimes, these can be good, like if you easily draw clear boundaries for how you want to be treated from the beginning of dating someone new. But other times, they can be holding you back from finding the love you want.

When I took that year off from dating, talking with a therapist and my best friend helped me to uncover the recurring choices I made that led to unhappy relationships. Since the men I dated were similar in the sense that they were cocky, opinionated, and not serious about a relationship, I concluded a few things from that observation: I looked for the approval of the men I dated (most likely because I had that dynamic with my dad as a child) and I couldn't be clear with the boundaries I needed to feel respected in a relationship. Both of those patterns left me feeling insecure and resentful towards my boyfriends. But, because I didn't even know those patterns existed, I continued on my merry way of repeating choices that left me feeling like crap.

Dating patterns exist subconsciously as beliefs and habits we collect over our lifetime: they come from experiences, our childhood, what we see in the media and other external sources. Once a belief functions within you on a subconscious level, it can be hard to break, just like any other habit. And even when I acknowledged my dating patterns for the pain they brought into my life, it took some trial and error to rid myself of them. Like the time I told my current boyfriend, Nish, I didn't want to date anymore. Back then, I wasn't ready to date a genuinely nice person. Luckily, I realized my mistake several months later.

It's important to realize and change your unhealthy dating patterns because you deserve healthy love that feels good. For me, the best part of taking a break from dating was identifying which dating patterns did me more harm than good. Sure, it took a conscious effort to change the way I dated, but acknowledging their presence was the first step to creating new patterns.

There are a few common dating patterns people fall victim to. They're not always easy to admit, but it'll do wonders for finding the kind of partner you've always deserved if you can be honest with yourself about whether you suffer from any of the following:

YOU CHANGE YOUR PERSONALITY TO PLEASE YOUR PARTNER

You don't feel comfortable being your genuine self in your relationship. You focus more on the type of person you think they want, rather than seeing if they accept you for you.

YOU AREN'T ABLE TO SPEAK UP ABOUT YOUR NEEDS

In turn, you find yourself feeling drained by the relationship emotionally, physically, and/or mentally. At some point, you may even resent your partner.

YOU PUSH PEOPLE AWAY, THINKING THEY'LL BREAK YOUR HEART

Because of this, you keep people at arm's length. You're worried that if you let your guard down, someone will hurt you. You end up sabotaging your relationships the moment things get serious and are afraid to commit to anyone.

YOU AREN'T ABLE TO MAKE COMPROMISES YOU ALWAYS FEEL LIKE YOUR WAY IS THE RIGHT WAY

You end up asserting your opinions to the extent that you create fights. You might even notice that your unwillingness to compromise is the reason your relationships tend not to move forward.

YOU DATE PEOPLE WHO GIVE YOU VALIDATION OF YOUR PLACE IN THIS WORLD

Doing this means your sense of self-worth is at the whim of the other person's behaviors. They might give you endless compliments one day or withhold them from you the next. Or, they could give you a healthy amount of affection, but no amount of reassurance ever feels good enough to you.

YOU MISTAKE A ROLLERCOASTER FOR LOVE

Fighting and tears make you feel like the relationship is thriving; you experience passion only during the highs or lows. You feel uncomfortable if things are going too well. You might even draw away from people who treat you with respect and kindness. You create arguments in an attempt to "liven" things up.

These are just a few common dating patterns people fall into. If you're still unsure whether you have dating patterns that hold you back from love, make two lists. On the first one, write out all the positive attributes of your past relationships. On another, write down all the negative aspects. Compare the two lists and mark any similarities you notice. Those are your patterns.

Sometimes, all of us need a little wake-up call to see we're the biggest obstacle standing in our way of love: romantic, self, or platonic. I could've kept dating similar men and blaming them for all my hurt feelings, but the reality was, I chose to bring those people into my life. It was clear that at least part of the problem was with my choices. That realization gave me hope; at least I held the power to make different decisions.

Once you have an understanding of your dating patterns, it's time to get down to the hard part. Remember how I said I dumped my boyfriend because I was still stuck in the allure of being attracted to jerks? Well, I sat with that choice for a while. I felt like I made a mistake. And months later, Nish and I reconnected at a mutual friend's going-away party. Even after we started dating again, I had to actively ignore that little voice telling me it was weird how nice Nish acted. I was used to mixed signals, but he was giving clear green signals. I worked on squashing that old dating pattern so I could fully accept what Nish was giving me. And I'm beyond glad I did.

Your journey to changing your dating patterns won't be easy, but changing any habit takes time. Just continue to be self-aware, patient, and remember these few things:

TIPS FOR CHANGING YOUR DATING PATTERNS:

- **Don't play games.** A relationship is like a house: you want to build on a solid foundation. Don't begin a relationship with someone who waits to text you back or goes silent for days. This isn't checkers, it's your love life.

- **Be forward about your intentions.** If the other person is turned off, then consider their reaction a blessing. You don't want to spend your precious time with someone who doesn't want the same things for the relationship as you.

- **Always prioritize yourself and your needs.** If you consistently stand strong in your values and needs from the people you date, then you won't feel like your boundaries have been overstepped.

- **Check in with yourself regularly.** Be honest about whether you're falling into your old dating patterns. If so, you need to decide if the relationship is worth continuing to pursue.

- **If a decision feels hard, it's probably what needs to be done.** Admitting you're ignoring your needs or falling into old ways means the solution will feel hard. That's because any type of growth will feel uncomfortable. But deep down, you know that it's the right thing to do.

- **Be open-minded to new ways of dating.** If the people you date end up hurting you, then it's important to be open to different types of people you may not normally go for. Dating new kinds of people might feel weird at first, but it could grow into the beautiful kind of love you've always wanted.

THIS IS WHY I DON'T BELIEVE IN SOULMATES

||||||||||

"The right person won't be perfect; they'll be the person wanting to learn the unique ways of your happiness. They'll be the one who is able to admit when they're wrong and promises to do better. The one who loves you no less even when you're the one who's wrong. Because the ability to learn, adapt, make mistakes, and grow with you throughout life will last longer than any illusion of a perfect partner you build up in your head that no one can live up to."

Y ou may believe in the idea that one day, you'll come across "the one." Your other half. Your ride or die. Your "soulmate," as many would say. If so, you're not alone; many people believe in the same sentiment of there being a single person out there who is meant to be with them. Hell, even I bought into this notion of destined love.

Remember my college boyfriend, Sean? The guy I met at a table read when he walked into the room with a James Dean-esque vibe? I thought Sean was my soulmate, but I couldn't have been more wrong.

As men came and went from my life, I started to wonder if love was as simple as two people destined to be together. I wanted to know more about how the term "soulmate" came to be, so I did some research on where the term came from.

The idea of a soulmate began in ancient Greece, when Plato wrote a fictional book on philosophers—like Socrates—discussing why love exists. When it was Aristophanes'—a famous comedian during that time—turn, he began describing to the room how humans once looked very different than they do now—with four arms, four legs, and two heads. These androgynous humans were powerful and threatened the sanctity of the gods. Worried about how mighty these humans could become, Zeus decided to use a lightning bolt and split the humans right down the middle, forming two separate people like we know today. After this split, the humans spent their lives longing for the other person they were separated from. And so, the idea of soulmates was born.

What a romantic thought, to believe we're destined to be with one specific person in this crazy world. I understand why people love the idea, but it's also clear the foundation of this story was merely a fun tale to entertain people. In reality, the idea of longing for only one person is a bit tragic. What if something bad were to happen to them? Or they found someone else before you? Or one day, you happened to miss the bus they were on because your neighbor wouldn't stop talking about their cats? Does that mean you're destined to be alone forever?

To be frank, the idea of a soulmate doesn't make any sense statistically. With billions of other people in this world, the odds of finding someone who you could fall in love with are probably higher than one single person. But that's not my biggest issue with soulmates. What worries me the most about the idea is the kind of expectations it puts on your partner. Can someone really be "perfect" for you? Is there such a thing as love at first sight? And, more importantly, is that the only kind of love there is?

The answers? No, no, and no.

I thought I fell in love with Sean the moment I laid eyes on him, but what I fell in love with was the idea of him (and his perfectly styled hair). Because soon enough, the illusion of our love began to fade. I noticed Sean criticized how he looked because of his job as an actor, and it was only a matter of time before he turned his aim at me. He pointed out everything he thought was a flaw in my body: from my cellulite to the fat in my arms. He told me I was dumb and couldn't fathom how I managed to get into college. And after a while of him treating me like I was his emotional punching bag, I began to treat him in the same way. My fantasy of our love shattered all around me. The truth was, we weren't destined to be together forever; we were only destined to be together for then.

The purpose of me explaining why soulmates aren't realistic isn't to discourage you. Actually, it's the complete opposite. I want to open your eyes to the fact that love is this messy thing with an imperfect human being that can grow, every day, into something even better. I want this insight to give you hope a happy relationship is out there for you.

BECAUSE THE TRUTH IS, YOU'LL NEVER COME ACROSS A PERSON WHO'S PERFECT. YOU'LL NEVER FIND A PARTNER WHO DOESN'T DISAPPOINT YOU AT ONE POINT.

Eventually, everyone will hurt you, even if it's an accident. Your partner will most likely get on your nerves, forget to put the toilet seat down, and get in arguments with you (but the good news is, that's actually healthy). Healthy relationships are between two people who can fix issues and grow together; not people who get along perfectly. And chances are, you won't know what that kind of love will look like.

You could feel butterflies from the beginning but be unsure about them for months, perhaps even years. Choosing to be vulnerable or spend your life with someone aren't decisions you should make lightly. You might need time to warm up to someone new. Or maybe you'll begin in an intense lustful passion that slowly levels out into a warm, nurturing love.

Maybe you'll find a person you're great with, but the world has different plans for you. Perhaps your careers will pull you apart or you won't see eye-to-eye on a fundamental aspect of your relationship. It's not that you lost your one chance at love; you will find it again, maybe even multiple times. Because with something as complex and mysterious as love, I refuse to believe we're only meant to fall into it with one specific person. Perhaps it will happen to you once, but chances are, you'll experience love multiple times throughout your life.

A soulmate was a cute story for Plato to write for entertainment, but give up your search for your one perfect partner. It's not realistic. What's realistic is finding an actual human being. Sure, they won't be your idea of perfection that you crafted throughout your life. But when you do find someone who you love, regardless of their faults, that's the moment you open yourself to real love, instead of the empty promises that the idea of a soulmate gives you.

LOVE IS MORE
THAN ROMANCE

||||||||||

"Love is something deeper than flowers,
fancy dinners, jewelry, or sex on the beach. Love
is more than a price tag or a one-time gesture.
Love happens in moments; it's built up through
choices and vulnerability. Love resides in the non-
physical experience between two people that can't
be measured but you know it when you're in it."

After dating many men, and finally finding my current boyfriend, Nish (who feels like an adventure and home wrapped into one), I've realized something important about love:

You might think love is someone running across the airport to tell you one last time how much they cherish you. You might believe love looks like flowers and rings and vacations and sweet nothings in your ear. You might think love and romance are the same, but they're far from it.

Romance is too simple to be the same thing as love, and that's what's so great about the latter. Love functions in a multitude of different ways that will continue to surprise you. But if you confuse romance for love, you could be hurt along the way.

Love may rush into you like a passionate whirlwind, but it might creep up on you as it did with Nish and me. I mentioned this earlier, but I was hesitant about this relationship at first. For me, loving Nish grew into my life, a plant growing roots and sprouting new leaves of memories and understanding along the way. For you, love may be your friend you never considered before. It may be the barista at your local coffee shop, the person doing yoga next to you in class. Love might not look the way you thought it would, but don't let a chance at a miraculous experience pass you by because it doesn't look like the ideas of romance you believe determines love.

LOVE EXISTS THROUGH THE HIGHS AND LOWS

Love may be repetitive at times; you'll wake up every day next to each other the same way you did yesterday and the day before. You'll make the bed and bump elbows while brushing your teeth. You'll go grocery shopping and the bills will never end. But in the routine bits is where you'll realize that love can last a lifetime; that there's no one else you'd rather be doing life's mundane tasks with. Because no one can ride the highs of love their whole life; passion is great and all, but live in it for more than a few days, and you'll become exhausted. Just like anything, love is bound to have its dull points. You'll watch the same show for the tenth time. You'll shop for paper towels or pick up their clothes every day. But these moments will feel like your favorite routine. Simply because you're doing it all with someone like them.

LOVE GROWS WITH EVERY COMPROMISE

You always hear people say, "nothing great comes easy," and the same goes for love: it'll be hard sometimes. You should feel respected and cherished, but love means compromising on whose family you spend Christmas with. It means arguments and talking about difficult feelings, like how you spend your money. It's admitting you're wrong and also learning to forgive when your partner accidentally hurts you. Love is something you work on, and the reward is wholly worth it; having a person to enjoy the smallest moments in life is worth the work.

LOVE IS HAVING SOMEONE SUPPORT YOU DURING HARD TIMES

There will be many people who stick around during the best times; you'll never have trouble finding people to celebrate with you. But coming across someone who stays, even when the lights turn off and life becomes hard, is the best feeling in the world. Real love sticks around for the good, the bad, and the not-so-Instagram-worthy.

LOVE IS RECIPROCAL

There's no, "what can you do for me?" but rather, "what can we do for each other?" Romance focuses on endlessly giving, even when it's not something the person can afford, whether that be monetarily or emotionally. Romance wants to enjoy your happiness and receive your admiration in the moment but it doesn't want the rest. It's self-satisfying and the exact opposite of how love functions. Love is a matter of balance between two people, when giving feels just as good as receiving.

I know that it's easy to get caught up in the whirlwind of feelings that come with romance. And by all means, please do so. There's nothing better than the rush of feelings running throughout your veins that comes with meeting someone new. But when the time comes that you're ready for lasting love, do not confuse the guise of romance for something more. While love can form out of romance, that doesn't always happen.

Love is so much more than anything you see in the movies; it's a lasting feeling, not an experience that ends once the credits start rolling.

PIECES OF DATING ADVICE THAT DO MORE HARM THAN GOOD

|||||||||

"There will come a time in your life where you need to question the beliefs you unconsciously picked up throughout life if you want to grow. You'll have to decide whether or not they serve you anymore based on where you want to be with your life. Because everyone is given beliefs about how to live, but that doesn't mean you need to keep them, especially when they're holding you back."

Y ou're going to hear a lot of dating advice throughout your life. While I'd like to think most people have good intentions, many people's words cause more harm than they realize.

Advice on dating is something that's been in our culture for generations. It's passed down like folklore from parents to children to cousins to friends. If you stop to think, I'm sure you can name a few people who tried to teach you a thing or two about the world of dating.

If it wasn't the people in your life, then perhaps it was the media who gave you your first lessons. For most of my childhood, I read magazines that wrote dating advice like it was the golden truth every young girl should follow. I believed every article I read: be charming, but not too funny. Act mysterious but not in a creepy way. Don't text too soon and always keep them guessing. If he makes fun of you on the first date, it means he likes you (gag). Those magazines were my only source for learning about how to find love, so why wouldn't I believe them?

Some dating advice is great, such as always meeting someone in public and trusting your gut. But a lot of dating advice is steeped in misguided ideas about when and how to find love. They focus too much on taking affection from others, instead of finding a relationship that feels authentic and lasting.

I lived my life guided by those popular pieces of dating advice for years and it proved to make my dating life complicated and stressful. I now realize dating shouldn't feel like this horrible part of your life that you need to get through as quick as possible. I blame crappy dating advice like the following for making people think that:

"WAIT TO TEXT THEM BACK"

There are two reasons why people think this works: you don't come off too anxious and you keep the other person guessing about your interest. But all I can think is, what kind of relationship are you setting yourself up for where someone wants to feel like they're not important to you? If you're dating someone who's weirded out when you text them back regularly, then they most likely aren't interested in you beyond a superficial fascination. If they genuinely enjoy communication that's sporadic and infrequent, then they'll continue to be like that all throughout a relationship.

"THEY'LL COME AROUND"

The hardest belief I had to rewire was believing you can make someone like you. That's just not the case. If a person is sending you "mixed signals" then that's a clear signal they're not interested. No amount of flirting or time will change that. And if you think you can change someone's mind, my question for you is: why do you think you're not worthy of someone's full interest? You shouldn't wait around in hopes someone will change their mind about you.

"IF THERE'S NO SPARK ON THE FIRST DATE, IT WASN'T MEANT TO BE"

Chances are, real love won't have a spark on the first date. A genuine connection can't be formed with a person over one dimly lit dinner on a Thursday night. It takes time to establish trust and interest in another person. I dated my boyfriend, ended things with him, and then tried giving dating another shot several months later before I realized how into Nish I was. Give second and third dates a chance.

"MAKE THEM WORK FOR YOU"

You might think having someone chasing you feels good because you're wanted, but that kind of dynamic will only last for so long. Sure, you should feel desired by someone, but so should your partner. A loving relationship is equal parts giving and receiving affection. If one person acts like they're better than the other, then things won't feel equal.

"YOU'RE BEING TOO PICKY"

While I think dating someone who's different from what you're used to can be a great way to shake up old dating patterns, only you know your boundaries and needs. Don't listen to others if they tell you you're being too picky; they're simply an outside opinion with no investment in your dating life. It's important to find a partner who treats you well, holds the same values as you, and with whom you feel a connection. Don't settle for less.

"AGE MATTERS"

Age doesn't matter nearly as much as other characteristics in a person. Emotional intelligence, respect, kindness, and the ability to grow with you rank much higher than age does. These qualities aren't determined by how long someone has lived, but rather, the way they were raised and the kind of experiences they've been through. I've dated men a decade older than me who didn't have the same maturity or integrity as someone two years younger than me.

FIRST DATE SIGNS THAT SOMEONE WON'T MAKE A GOOD PARTNER

||||||||||

"An illusion can only exist so long as the other person doesn't take a step closer to determine for themselves if things are as they appear."

D ating should be a fun process, but you're bound to come across people who ruin your hopes in it. I'm talking about the people who ghost or try to pressure you into moving too quickly (or maybe something unbearable like bad B.O.). Finding someone you want to be in a relationship with shouldn't be riddled with stress and anxiety, but I'd be lying if I said that, without a doubt, dating will always be fun.

But I will say dating is a vulnerable process no matter how you do it. When feelings get involved in meeting someone new, it can be hard to clearly see all the red flags the person sitting in front of you is waving. You might be on a date worrying if there's broccoli in your teeth or focusing on not falling off a wobbly stool at a bar. Meanwhile, your date is on their best behavior because they're hoping to impress you. That's why it's not easy to spot if someone isn't a good person during the first few dates; showing their worst qualities up-front would mean some people would be single forever. Yet it's one of the worst feelings in the world to be dating someone for weeks, start to really like them, and then realize they're a jerk just acting like a nice person.

Two relationships before I took my year break from dating, I met up with an old co-worker, Jack. We grabbed drinks and reminisced on our days at the old office; we were the first hires at a start-up snack company. Working there was like an all-hands-on-deck experience rather than sticking to our job titles since there were only four people in the company. Jack and I became close during my year with the company (not romantically... yet), simply because it was just us two for a while.

I sat across from Jack sipping on my glass of Merlot in a dress I bought in Venice Beach. We talked about old coworkers and at that time we went out in New Orleans on a work trip. I joked that I thought Jack was going to hit on me in Louisiana, which he didn't deny (even though he had a girlfriend at the time). It felt like two friends just catching up until it didn't. The way Jack's eyes glistened when he told me I looked good was the first time I thought maybe he was flirting with me. He joked in his usual manner: cocky, brash, and sometimes at my expense. But I let it all slide because that was just how Jack was. If anything, I was buying into his allure; the simple fact he was eleven years older than me made the whole idea of us together sexier. At the end of the night, while walking me to my car, he grabbed my hand. He spun me around and kissed me without the slightest hesitation. I pressed my lips back against his, even though I felt like something was off the moment our mouths touched.

I could feel in my gut that things with Jack weren't right, but I chose to ignore that feeling like I always did. We continued to date, and I continued to romanticize the idea of dating someone with whom I'd been friends for a while. It's like we had a head start on our relationship, I thought to myself.

The relationship was far from a smooth progression. Jack was hesitant about making the relationship anything serious—even texting me to say we shouldn't date but then taking it back a few weeks later. My friends expressed their worry about me dating Jack; his cocky attitude unsurprisingly came off as rude, more often than not. Rather than listen to their warnings, though, I carried on dating him, regardless of the fact we always disagreed and our values were wildly different.

As time progressed, I couldn't ignore that parts of Jack's personality made my skin crawl. His jokes about women weren't light-hearted, they were misogynistic. On more than one occasion, Jack made remarks that were blatantly racist. Once I started hanging out at his apartment more, I realized he drank a lot. Every night he prepared at least two old-fashioneds, grabbing at any chance to get drunk off his ass, which I didn't think too much into at the time; he was a more loving version of himself when he drank, anyway.

By the time I admitted to myself how blatantly different our values in life were, I felt too invested in the relationship to let go of it. I decided to just talk to him about all of my concerns, rather than leave him. And while I'm glad I spoke up, the relationship didn't last much longer before Jack pulled the trigger on our inevitable breakup.

Looking back on our first few dates—or even when we were simply co-workers—the signs were obvious that Jack wouldn't make a good boyfriend for me. His behaviors didn't bother me when we were working together. On our first dates, the mystery of "will this turn into something more?" distracted me from noticing his crude remarks. I didn't see—or chose to ignore—the signs.

First dates are an interesting situation because people are on their best behavior, which I don't fault them for. But then there are the people who take it a step further and act beyond just being nice; they deceive their dates, usually because of their own unresolved issues. I don't want to discourage you, but the reality is, if there are any red flags on the first few dates, you need to notice the signs because things will only get worse from there. While some people can hide their worst traits, there are still signs you can look out for to tell if someone isn't a genuinely good person. You just have to take notice if your date does any of the following:

THEY WERE RUDE TO THE WAITER

Someone who is rude to people they consider "below them," or someone who has a hierarchy mentality at all, isn't a kind-hearted person. It might seem innocent that your date made a joke about the hostess, but that's a major red flag. If your date is willing to make fun of a stranger, imagine how the tables will turn on you once they're not on their, what I call, "first date best behavior."

IT FELT LIKE THE NIGHT WAS CONTROLLED BY THEM

Did your date ask you questions, or did they mostly talk about themselves? Were they insisting they knew what is best to order? Did they boast about their life, even when you didn't ask?

If someone acts this way, it might indicate they're a controlling person or highly ego-driven. If they're already acting like this on the first date, that kind of behavior will only get worse over time.

THEY TRIED TO PRESSURE YOU INTO INTIMACY

There's no right or wrong decision when it comes to kissing or sleeping with someone on the first date, as long as you feel comfortable. But there's something to worry about if you decline someone's advances and they continue to insist. That person isn't respecting a boundary you've clearly drawn for them. And when it comes to sexual safety, that's pretty important for a solid relationship.

THEY BROUGHT UP THEIR EX, MULTIPLE TIMES

Sometimes, people don't move on from their exes as quickly as they'd like to, and that's fine. But if they're bad-mouthing their ex on a first date, that's not okay. It might seem harmless to hear about their "crazy" ex, but usually that's only half the story. Usually, there's another side to the narrative and it's the part where your date isn't as innocent as they seem.

THEY MADE REMARKS THAT OFFENDED YOU

When your date makes a racist/sexist/elitist remark to you, take that at face value. It's not a joke; it's a sign of their true character. You're not being sensitive by feeling offended, you're in tune with your morals. If this happens, don't be afraid to speak up and leave.

THEIR OPINIONS FELT OVERPOWERING

No two people will ever have the exact same opinions. When it comes to a relationship, there's nothing wrong with thinking differently. But, to form a healthy one in which both people feel respected, you have to know how to handle someone's opinions that are different from yours. From the get-go, if your date belittles your views or tries to change your mind, they're not going to respect your opinions further down the road.

MAKING FIRST DATES FUN AGAIN

||||||||||

"It's a beautiful thing to meet a new person; someone with volumes of life stories you have yet to read. Don't be scared of finding out what those chapters contain. Rather, venture in with curiosity and know that just because you didn't finish it until the end means that book was a waste of your time."

First dates always made me nervous. On top of the general worry of, *this person might be a serial killer,* I over-planned my outfits and over-thought everything that could go wrong.

Once when I was single, I decided to try a yoga studio near my house that offered the first class free to new clients. I signed up for a morning hot vinyasa class and felt good for the first ten minutes. Then, I started feeling light-headed and had to step into the lobby for some fresh air. While I cooled down, the receptionist offered me some water. He was a tall, yoga-built brunette named Sam who had the cutest smile. We talked for a while until the class I was taking ended. I slipped into the studio to grab my mat. When

I came back out, the lobby was filled with students signing in for the next class. I slipped out the door and started walking home.

I instantly regretted not asking Sam for his number; he was cute, charming, and a yogi... how could I have passed that up? I called one of my friends and told her the story, emphasizing what an idiot I was for missing my chance to ask him out on a date.

"Call the studio!" she exclaimed, which I said would be crazy to do. But after thinking about it a bit, I figured, why the hell not. What did I have to lose?

I called the studio and Sam immediately answered (I almost hung up). I explained I was the girl who popped out of the morning vinyasa class that day because I felt sick. He remembered me; a good sign. I asked him if he wanted to go to dinner sometime. Sam paused for a moment and then said he'd love to and that he was impressed I called the studio to ask him out; double score.

Sam and I made plans to grab dinner at a local Italian restaurant the next night. All day I felt anxious about our date. I must've tried on ten outfits, worried about my limited knowledge of yoga, and wondered if Sam would think I was interesting enough compared to the beautiful yogis he was always surrounded by (notice that lack of self-worth).

During the date, my nerves didn't calm down. I felt like I was talking weird because I apparently forgot how to eat noodles and speak at the same time. Everything I did felt awkward and it was hard to hear Sam talk because of the restaurant's loud music. But from the amount I did catch, Sam wasn't as much of the yogi as I thought he was. Turns out, he was more into gaming than yoga. "I just took the job because I needed some money," he said.

Let me be clear: I have nothing against gaming. My current man is literally gaming as I type this chapter. But Sam's lack of direction or ambition in life was a turn off I couldn't ignore.

We finished dinner and Sam walked me to my car. I could feel the tension begin to build as the part of the night that gives me the most anxiety neared closer: whether or not he'd try to kiss me. I didn't think the date went that well, but I also wasn't the best at creating the boundary of saying no to a kiss. Our night ended with a way-too-long make out session against my car. After that, there was no second date.

I must've gone on at least twenty dates before I stopped to wonder why I didn't really like first dates. Some of my friends loved them but, like me, a lot of them didn't. I thought, "why do first dates fill me with dread?" And after considering all my good and bad first dates, I came to the realization of one fact about myself: I cared way too much if the other person enjoyed the date, rather than if I had fun.

A lot of people feel a similar sentiment. Dating advice in magazines and articles heavily focus on whether the other person likes you. So much so that we completely forget to actually have fun ourselves. I know that finding someone to be in a relationship with is important to a lot of people, and it was to me, too. But how are we ever supposed to put our best selves forward if we're caught up in our nerves?

Dating is just as much about enjoying the process as it is you deciding if you enjoy your date's company. Only focusing on if the other person likes you or thinks you're a good match ends up doing you a disservice in the long run.

I want you to imagine how your dates typically go. What kind of emotions do you feel? Happy? Nervous? Judgmental? Anxious? If it's anything but a positive experience, why are you continuing down the same path that doesn't make you feel good? You don't have to give up dating, but maybe it's time to consider a different mindset around first dates.

BEGIN WITH RE-FRAMING HOW YOU THINK ABOUT BEING SINGLE

Being single isn't this terrible affliction brought onto you. It's not a stamp on your forehead labeling you as damaged goods. If someone talks about your singledom as this sad story, they're projecting their own fears of being alone onto you. People have all sorts of reasons for being single; some even choose the single life voluntarily. Thinking there's something wrong with you simply because you don't have a partner is buying into the idea that your worth is determined by another person.

DON'T DEFAULT TO DRINKS OR DINNER

If drinking isn't really your thing (it's never been mine) or grabbing dinner is getting old, mix it up. I never understood why everyone automatically chooses dinner as a first date. I mean, food is great and all, but I feel awkward when I'm eating in front of someone new. Instead, opt for something you like doing. Ask your date if they want to go to a museum or maybe a concert. Bring them into your world by doing something you enjoy, so you can see how they fare. Bonus: you'll enjoy the night, too.

HAVE A BIT OF FUN GETTING READY

There's no need to tense up before a first date as I did, even if you're super excited. In my experience, sitting around waiting until it's time to call an Uber is a sure way to work up your nerves. Instead, spend more time getting ready for the date. Take a bubble bath and play your favorite music. Try on a bunch of outfits until you find one you feel confident in. Watch a TV show you love or read a book up until the moment you have to leave.

SHOW UP ACTING LIKE YOURSELF, STRAIGHT FROM THE BEGINNING

It's exhausting trying to act in a way you think your date would like. Plus, you're not dating to try and please everyone. Instead, act like your authentic self from the moment you say hi. Behave like you would if you were with a friend. Because for now, at the very least, a first date is like establishing a friendship. And the best kind of relationships start from a friendship (most of the time; I'm looking at you, Jack).

TALK ABOUT THINGS YOU'RE BOTH INTERESTED IN

If your date mentions he's into painting miniature action figures (true story), then ask more about the process. What made them get into that hobby? Is it hard to use a tiny paintbrush to fill in the details? You'll find the best part of a person shine through when they're talking about the things they love. The same goes for you, too. Don't be afraid to tell a story that happened to you recently that was funny or exciting. Describe your hobbies with the same excitement you would when talking to your friends.

LOWER YOUR EXPECTATIONS, A LOT

Sure, it only takes one date to find a great relationship, but that'll happen when it's meant to. Not every date is going to be extraordinary. Lower your expectations so that, at the very least, you enjoy the date for what it is. Even if the person isn't your idea of "the one," which I hope by now you don't subscribe to, they can at least be a fun person to spend your night with. Once you lower your expectations for the date (not your ideal person), you'll feel less pressure. And who knows, maybe that person will surprise you.

DON'T BE AFRAID TO END A BAD DATE

You're not obligated to see a date through if it's not going well. You'll become jaded if you stay for a bunch of bad dates, wishing you were elsewhere. Give the date a solid chance, but if someone shows up looking nothing like their dating profile or offends you in some way, you have every right to end things early. Politely say you need to leave and don't look back (just don't forget to grab your jacket and phone, first).

LET YOUR DATE KNOW IF YOU'RE HAVING A GOOD TIME

You're both bound to be nervous on a first date, especially if you like each other. Break the ice by letting the other person know you're enjoying the night. A simple, "I'm having a lot of fun," can diffuse any tension that may have built up from wondering what the other person is thinking.

MIXED SIGNALS ARE A CLEAR SIGNAL

||||||||||

"Words are just that.
You've spent too much of your life holding
on to the noises that were uttered so effortlessly
by people who didn't act on them.

You need action.
You need gestures.
You deserve more than empty promises."

If there's one thing that would drive anyone crazy, it's having someone you're interested in be unclear with how they feel about you. This looks like someone saying they missed you but never replying to your texts about locking down a date to hang out. Maybe the guy you went to the movies with last week watched your Instagram story but didn't reply to your text that morning. Perhaps it's that someone acts like your partner but avoids ever talking about being exclusive; they use the line "they're just a friend" when they mention you to other people.

It's what the world of modern dating dubbed "mixed signals."

Going back to when I dated my 11-years-older-than-me ex-co-worker, Jack, we didn't go from dating to a relationship smoothly. In fact, once we started hanging out regularly and things were clearly becoming more serious, he had quite the response.

Jack moved to Marina Del Rey—a beautiful beach city in Los Angeles with sailboats constantly in sight—right before we began dating. I knew he was excited about the move after living in Hollywood (an area of LA that seems great in the movies but isn't so great to live in). I'd spent the night at Jack's new apartment a few times and by now, we hung out regularly. That is, until he sent me a text message.

"I think you're great and I obviously want to be friends still, but I kinda want to be free to date other people. I just moved to Marina Del Rey and I want to see what kind of ladies are out there on the beaches," he said.

I kid you not.

I let Jack drag me along for two months to what I thought would be a relationship. Turned out, having me sleep over all the time and regularly going on dinner dates wasn't serious in his mind.

I'll be the first to say: I should've run for the damn hills when I got that text. Sadly, our story didn't end there, and I let myself fall back into the trap of dating and wondering what Jack's intentions were. He was the king of mixed signals: planning dates all the time and having me sleep over. I was the queen of thinking I could ignore all the crappy things he did, like that "ladies on the beaches" message.

All this is to say, I understand why people put up with shoddy messaging and erratic behavior. Mixed signals keep people lying awake at night, trying to decipher why someone they're interested in is always "busy." They're the reason people screenshot their messages and send them to a group chat, asking their friends for a second opinion on whether or not someone is into them.

Mixed signals cause a lot of anxiety and confusion, but really, there shouldn't be any confusion at all. Mixed signals are a clear signal: the person doesn't want to be serious with you.

Whether it's because they see you as a friend or someone they don't want to commit to, mixed signals are a clear indicator of someone's lack of interest.

WHEN IT COMES DOWN TO IT, IF SOMEONE IS INTO YOU, THEY'LL LET YOU KNOW

I should've seen that with Jack. That if he wanted a relationship, he would've pursued me like he did the "ladies on the beaches." Even if the person you're dating is a bit shyer, you at least know their texts won't be sporadic, and they'll make an effort to see you.

Think about when you're really into someone. You most likely text them throughout the week, make plans to go see a movie; the communication flows. You're interested in what's going on in that person's world. You get to know more about each other. You're not DMing them once every two weeks and assuming that suffices.

I know it's hard to move on from someone you like, but the other choice is to continue to allow them to treat you as less than you deserve. If that's what you're currently struggling with, then you should ask yourself, "Why don't I believe I deserve someone who wants me as much as I want them?"

Sure, the people who manipulate others' emotions are part of the issue but you're the one choosing to keep them in your life. You're telling them it's okay to treat you like this, so why would they act differently?

Dating doesn't have to be this hard. Love shouldn't feel like a game of cat and mouse. There are many people in the world who would love to be in a relationship with you. The decision to move on from someone sending you mixed signals is one only you can make and these tips will help you do that.

YOU NEED TO HAVE BOUNDARIES TO ENSURE YOUR EMOTIONAL SAFETY

Boundaries are important in any relationship, but even more so when it comes to dating. They allow you to move through the dating process while still maintaining your values and respect from your dates.

You need to decide for yourself what kind of behaviors you're willing to put up with and which ones you're not. Are you tired of someone avoiding a conversation about making your relationship more serious? Do you expect honesty, rather than one lie after the next? Once someone violates your boundaries, it's hard to build a relationship on that kind of rocky foundation.

IF YOU THINK THERE MAY BE A VIABLE EXCUSE, ASK

If the person starts acting weird, then chances are they're aware of how they're acting. In which case, you have every right to ask what's up. Maybe a work or family emergency happened that they felt awkward bringing up. If that's true, you can clear the air rather than continuing to wonder what's going on. But be cautious; if they keep making reasons to not see you, their excuses are just that, excuses.

REFOCUS THAT ENERGY ON SOMETHING PRODUCTIVE

I can write all day long condemning mixed signals and insisting you deserve more, but it's hard to take that advice right away. Let's at least agree that reeling over someone's lack of texting back isn't going to help the situation. So instead of leaping at your phone anytime you hear it vibrate, shift that energy into something that'll distract your mind.

Finish the errands you've had on your list for weeks. Tackle a house project you've been wanting to start. Invest more time in hobbies you love. Journal all of your feelings out until your heart feels lighter. Use your energy on something that's going to make you feel a bit better about yourself and help you forget your dating dilemma.

REMIND YOURSELF OF YOUR WORTH

You're a person worthy of respect and love. You don't need to settle for someone who treats you like you're a second thought. The right person won't make you question your worth. They won't make you wonder where you stand with them. They'll let you know how much you mean to them.

Modern dating is an interesting time to find love in. We're more connected than ever, but that makes people flakier and less willing to commit because it's easy to hide behind a phone. You have to look out for yourself first and be wary of people who aren't genuine. Just remember, the right person will let you know they're into you. Mixed signals are clear signals they're not the right person.

ACTIONS TO HELP YOU DETERMINE IF YOU'RE SOMEONE'S PRIORITY

||||||||||

"The truth is simple: someone who doesn't invest the same energy into you that you invest into them isn't someone you couldn't be enough for. They're simply a person who wasn't meant to be in your life beyond this point."

Let me say this loud and clear: wanting to be a priority in someone's life isn't a bad thing (notice I said "a" and not "their top"). When you like someone and see a potential future with them, it's natural to want those feelings to be reciprocated. One way of determining if that's the case is whether they prioritize you.

I had a very scary incident happen back when I worked as a pet sitter three years ago. It shed light on how much of a priority I was to the guy I was dating, Brandon. He was my best friend's roommate at the time. We'd known each other for about a year before we tried dating. Our relationship started out on a rocky foundation because my previous relationship with Jack ended a mere month before. We constantly stepped on each other's toes during the duration of our relationship but felt the intense passion in between. We'd go from making out at concerts to him ignoring me for a week because he "needed to think."

During this time, I'd recently left my job as a technical recruiter. I opted to work part-time as a nanny while I figured out what career I wanted to pursue. On top of nannying, I advertised in my town that I was available to pet sit, even overnight. A family contacted me, after seeing I was a USC alum and decided to hire me to watch their white Maltese. His dog had a health condition that required medication at night and in the morning and because of that, part of the job required me to sleep over at the house when the family was out of town.

On the first night of ever staying at the house, I was upstairs in their daughter's bedroom, watching TV. I heard a creaking noise that sounded just like a door opening. Since it was nighttime and the house was big, I couldn't see anything when I looked down the hallway. I stood in the room, a little worried about what I heard, when another creaking noise started. It sounded like movement in the house. At this point, I called Brandon.

He brushed off my worry as me overreacting. He said to calm down and he was busy watching a movie. I felt embarrassed and hung up the phone. But then I heard the same noise of a door, without a doubt, opening.

I called my best friend, Dannie, who happened to be watching a movie with Brandon and his friend at their house. He took my call in the other room while I cried into the phone about how scared I was. "Breathe. It's ok. You need to hang up the phone and call the cops," Dannie calmly stated.

I ended our call and dialed 911. The operator had me give the address of the house and told me to shut and barricade the door. He stayed on the phone with me as local police came out to the property. I saw the blue and red lights flash from the street and a few seconds later I heard one cop come into the house and yell "THIS IS THE POLICE."

That cop and two others searched the home. They went into every single room before clearing that no one in the house but me. Just as the officers were leaving, one of the men said to me, "Just make sure you close the back door. It was wide open." But the thing was, I never opened the back door.

Later, Dannie told me he tried to get Brandon to drive him to come to check on me at the house. Brandon told him, "She's fine. She's making a big deal out of nothing." It was at that moment I realized how low of a priority I was on Brandon's list. I felt hurt and like my feelings were taken for granted. I couldn't understand Brandon's reaction to all of this. "I'd never treat someone like that," I thought to myself.

If you're worried the person you're dating doesn't prioritize you either, chances are, you're putting a solid amount of effort into the relationship (or whatever it is you two are doing). It's a crappy feeling when the other person doesn't do the same. It leaves you wondering if there's something wrong with you even though, spoiler, nothing is wrong with you.

Sometimes, you're part of someone's priorities. But other times, you simply aren't a priority at all. When it's the latter, it means you should move on, find someone who will prioritize you, and stop wasting your time on someone who doesn't deserve it.

Here are a few actions you can look out for to tell if you aren't someone's priority:

THEY CANCEL ON YOU, OFTEN

Have you gotten to the point where you assume there's a 50/50 chance you'll see them when you make plans? Does the person you're dating seem to always have an "emergency" or something that "came up?" Or are they regularly late? After someone cancels on you several times, their excuses are merely excuses. The reality is that something they see as a better opportunity probably came up, whether that be drinks with their friends or hitting the gym.

A guy I once dated made excuse after excuse as to why he couldn't meet up for our dates. They continued to pile up until he called me one day to say he didn't want to date anymore. He explained he wasn't ready for a relationship yet got into a new one within the month.

I don't hold a grudge against him; that's just the way things go. Not everyone works out. But I could've avoided a lot of sadness if I'd recognized his flakiness as a sign I wasn't a priority to him.

YOU'VE NEVER MET THEIR BEST FRIEND

When someone's excited to date you, they want to show you off. Some people are hesitant about introducing a new relationship to their family (which is reasonable), so their best friend is usually their go-to person to introduce the new person they're seeing to.

If you've been dating each other or been in a relationship for months and you haven't met their best friend, something might be up (FaceTime or even a phone call counts if it seemed purposeful). I can't tell you for sure whether or not they're keeping you a secret, so if it bothers you, bring it up. There's a chance the opportunity hasn't come up, but it might also be they think you won't be around for long, so they don't see a point in introducing you to other people.

YOU WOULDN'T FEEL COMFORTABLE CALLING THEM IN AN EMERGENCY

Our intuitions are pretty spot-on. When something seems fishy, our minds often get in the way saying things like, "they're just busy," or "they're not good at texting." But in our gut, we know the truth. So, ask yourself this: would you feel comfortable calling them in an emergency? Or would you be worried they wouldn't answer/care/help?

Right before I decided to call Brandon for help during the pet sitting incident, I hesitated. I didn't want to feel like a burden, and even then, I knew he wouldn't have a good reaction. My intuition was that he'd write me off, and that's exactly what happened.

That's why I love this exercise. If you don't feel comfortable calling the person you're dating (given you've been going on dates regularly) in an emergency, there's a reason you're not comfortable making that call.

YOUR COMMUNICATION EXISTS SOLELY ON DMS

Let's be real: communication that exists exclusively through DMs isn't the kind of communication that speaks to a serious relationship. I have conversations with my friends all the time on Instagram, but they're light-hearted and fun. Meaningful communication happens via texts or, better yet, phone calls. If someone only hits you up on your DMs, they're essentially saying, "Hey, I only thought of you because you popped up on my Instagram story."

For someone to text, you have to come to their mind naturally throughout the day. They have to go into their messages, find your name, and craft a text. It might not be a lot of effort, but it's a lot more than a slide into your DMs.

THEY AVOID FIGHTS OR GIVE IN TO YOUR SIDE

Arguments take work. Fights are draining. I've avoided starting many discussions or debates with acquaintances because I didn't care much about us coming to an understanding. I'd rather ignore it altogether than feel exhausted after an argument.

Someone who doesn't prioritize you in their life will do the same. They want fun. They want easy. What they don't want is a long conversation about how them ignoring you for three days was messed up.

When someone takes the time to have a serious conversation with you, whether that be an argument or discussion, that's a sign they care on some level. They're not just in it for the fun emotions; they want to work through the serious ones, too.

YOU'RE THE LAST PERSON TO HEAR ABOUT A MAJOR LIFE EVENT

Has the person you're dating ever casually mentioned something major like moving into a new apartment or receiving a promotion? Did it feel more accidental than on purpose? Does that happen a lot?

It's because they don't see you as someone who they want to tell important news to.

Think back to the last time you were excited about something. Who did you call? Your best friend? Mom? Co-worker? Boyfriend (at the time)?

You chose who you prioritize most in life. That's what the person you're dating does, too. If you're finding out about major life events way down the road, it's a sign that you're not very important to them.

Not being a priority to someone you care about can feel demoralizing and altogether confusing. If you invest energy into a relationship, it's normal to want the other person to do the same.

But the good news is, if you're not a priority in someone's life, you can always leave and find someone who will prioritize you.

ON WHAT LOVE ISN'T

IIIIIIIIII

"Just because you can't see it doesn't mean love isn't everywhere. You cannot see air, yet you know it fills your lungs and gives you life. You cannot see gravity yet here you are, fastened to the Earth's surface. Yes, you cannot see love, yet you'd do anything for someone who doesn't share your blood. You pursue your passions until your body is exhausted. Your senses light up at the mere sight of the sun's rays across a flower. You keep choosing someone, even when you wake up next to them just like you do every day. You might not be able to hold, touch, or see love, but you can experience it all around you when you take the time to stop and notice it."

I love to write about love, so much so that I made a career out of it. As a result, I think about love all the time. In the shower. On walks. When I look at my boyfriend while he's asleep in the morning (not creepy in a creepy way, of course). I often wonder about the nature of love. How does it form? How does one describe the feeling? What are the symptoms? And is everyone's experience of love the same?

I like to explain the definition of love as describing a color. You can't, really. You can point at a nearby tree and say, "That's green," but describing the color always leads to further comparisons.

This same phenomenon goes for love. You can read novels and listen to songs. You can notice a couple pass by you on the sidewalk and assume they're in love. You can watch romantic movies that make you feel warm and good inside, maybe even bring a tear to your eye.

BUT EVERYONE JUST GUESSES AS TO WHAT LOVE IS, EVEN ME.

I've been in relationships where I thought I was in love. Then I began new relationships and realized the former wasn't love; it was just another feeling I mistook for love.

All anyone can do is guess at what love might be through experience, error, and vulnerability. That can seem scary, putting your heart out there, unsure of where it might land. But when you do find the elusive experience of love, you'll realize the journey was worth it.

And luckily, along that journey, you can at least know what love *isn't* and through that realize what love most likely looks like for you.

LOVE ISN'T A GAME

Love isn't about keeping score. It's not a back and forth of who last showed their emotions, or who won the last fight. There's no time to wait to text back and no reason to act like you don't care. Love is being on one team. You may disagree, but your goal is the same. You want the best for one another and the relationship. Playing games when it comes to matters of the heart is destructive and cruel.

LOVE ISN'T FORCED

Love can't be coerced. It's not something you can make someone feel. Forcing love won't lead to someone feeling what was never there. It'll lead to an act; interest, maybe. Pity, at worst.

Love appears naturally, at its own time. It's not always easy, but there's no question of whether either person wants to be in love. You both make plans to see each other; you both make the effort to be in one another's lives.

LOVE ISN'T WANTING TO CONSTANTLY RIP SOMEONE'S CLOTHES OFF

Love isn't lust and it's not carnal. Wanting to get in bed with someone because they're irresistibly attractive isn't love. No matter the passion. No matter the sexual chemistry.

Love is deeper than what you can see in a photo. It's being attracted to their looks, sure, but it's also being drawn to the essence of who they are. Love is being intimate, on more levels than just sexual.

LOVE ISN'T RUSHING THROUGH MILESTONES

Love isn't a race. It's not measured by how quickly you move in together. Your devotion is not determined by what age you walk down the aisle. Milestones are celebrations, not something to get to as quickly as possible.

Love unfolds at its own pace. It's the sense of security with one another that you'll make decisions when you're both ready. You don't compare your love to others' timelines because you know your love is unique to you.

LOVE ISN'T BECOMING ONE

Love isn't about finding the person who completes you. It's not about enmeshing with your partner to become one. Love isn't two halves coming together to form a whole.

Love is about being complete on your own. It's encouraging that same wholeness in your partner. Your love is made stronger by being the best version of yourselves, and you both support that individuality.

LOVE ISN'T OWNERSHIP

Love isn't making everyone know the other person is "yours". It's not someone trying to control who you see, how you spend your time and your life outside of the relationship.

Love is respecting your partner's life even when you're not involved. It's knowing you're both individuals with differences that are respected. You don't belong to each other; instead, you choose to be with each other. And this free will in love is part of what makes it beautiful.

LOVE ISN'T CONDITIONAL

Love isn't expecting things to fit into a neat box. It's not loving one day and withholding affection the next because you're upset.

Love is messy. It's accepting that sometimes you'll have bad days and so will your partner. It's supporting each other through those hard times, instead of hurting one another. Love that's meant to last will stick with you through the good and bad times.

LOVE ISN'T PAINFUL

Love isn't throwing word daggers at your partner. It's never intentionally trying to cause the other pain. It's not manipulation or humiliation.

Love is about helping one another avoid pain. It's realizing that sometimes you'll accidentally hurt the other person and apologizing because that wasn't your intention. Love is enjoying happiness together, not creating pain for one another.

LOVE ISN'T THE END OF THE STORY

Love isn't about reaching a happily ever after. There's no end goal to work to get to. Love is the present. It's working through obstacles that come your way. It's choosing to care for your partner every day. You both know the journey doesn't end at the aisle or the first "I love you"; that's where it all continues.

LOVE ISN'T PERFECT

Love isn't pristine and shiny. It's not fight-free. Love won't come in a neatly packaged box with clear instructions on how to proceed forward.

Love is arguing and disagreeing. It's learning to admire each other in new ways when your partner surprises you, growing with one another as you inevitably change throughout life. Love is an adventure of unknowns (the good, the bad, the stumbles) that you wouldn't want to do with anyone else.

THE MOST UNDERRATED QUALITIES THAT MAKE A GREAT PARTNER

IIIIIIIIII

*"May you be someone's first choice; someone's
only choice, someone's best choice."*

If someone were to ask you to describe your ideal partner, what would you list? Maybe things like attractive, funny, tall, or sweet. While all those qualities are great, I feel like they miss a deeper, underlying vein that runs through the best relationships; qualities we weren't taught make for a great partner but do.

When I was younger, if I were asked to describe my ideal boyfriend, my list would've been similar to the one above. I cared about dating a guy I thought was funny and exuded confidence. I always imagined I'd be with a very tall, sandy blonde haired man. I was determined to find an outdoorsy guy, even though I'm not much of the camping type.

But when I took a step back from dating and started to be more aware of what aspects of a partner made me happiest, I realized those aspects of a person came pretty low on my list or were completely erased. The surface-level qualities I looked for like blonde hair and being an outdoorsy kind of guy made zero difference in whether or not someone would be a great partner.

When I began dating my current boyfriend, Nish, I was surprised how the qualities I valued in him—exceptional communication skills, kindness to every person he knows—were things I never considered in the past. Nish is a beautiful melting pot of many qualities that make me feel comfortable and that I didn't even know I valued in a partner. Because, like many aspects of life, we can't know what we need or what makes us happiest until we experience it. In the meantime, we're stuck thinking big muscles and a cute face will make for the best partner because it's what we saw on *Gossip Girl* or *Lizzie McGuire*.

It's time everyone stops going blindly down the same road of chasing qualities in a partner that aren't what would make for a thriving relationship. I want you to stop and consider what qualities in a person bring you joy or bring out the best in you? If you're not sure, take it from what I learned after making poor choices in love; there are several underrated qualities in a partner that make for the best relationships:

EMOTIONAL INTELLIGENCE

Emotional intelligence, also known as EQ, was always a quality I admired in myself. As a dating and relationship writer who focuses on human connections, deep-diving into my own feelings and learning how to put them into words is the biggest part of what I do.

Yet, I continued to date men who had the emotional depth of a teaspoon.

Whenever I'd talk about my feelings, it either overwhelmed or freaked out the men I chose to date. In both of those cases, things never ended well. Often, I'd be gaslighted (made to feel crazy) for experiencing normal human emotions, or put through the classic move of them ignoring me all together.

When I met Nish, he made it clear that nothing was ever off the table. He'd rather have the same conversation over and over until things were cleared up than for me to keep my feelings from him. And though Nish isn't the best at expressing his own emotions, he is hell-bent on becoming better with practice (another quality I admire in him).

EQ is the capacity to be aware of, control, and express one's feelings. It's also someone's awareness of how their actions impact other people. Instead of bottling up or ignoring their feelings, people with a high EQ have the words and awareness to talk about their emotions when they experience them.

If you've been in a few relationships before, you probably know how much people struggle to put words to what they're feeling. You might even know people who bottle up their emotions until they burst out as feelings of resentment. Not everyone is taught how to healthily express their emotions. Maybe their family ignored them when they showed emotions or punished them for crying in public.

While some people may have work to do to get back in touch with their feelings, the good news is, anyone can raise their EQ. Finding a partner with either a high EQ or willingness to increase theirs is like winning the lottery, trust me on that one. Life is a long journey, with inevitable bumps along the way. You don't want someone who causes themselves and you pain because they refuse to talk about what they're experiencing. Having a partner who can communicate their feelings and express appreciation for you is going to make for a relationship that can withstand whatever happens down the road.

THE ABILITY TO GROW WITH YOU

During my break from dating, I became obsessed with a show called *Parenthood*. My friend who's a therapist recommended it to me because she said it's a sweet and humble show. After a tumultuous breakup, I needed a bit of humble in my rather unstable life.

Parenthood follows a family in Northern California. It centers around two grandparents, Zeek and Camille, and follows their four adult kids, and all of their grandchildren. Throughout the show, the families go through various realistic struggles. The common thread is always the grandparents: a solid support system that seemed unbreakable.

But towards the end of the series, Camille expresses that she's tired of holding everyone together and wants to take art classes in Italy. She feels stuck in a life that's been the same for decades; no one appreciates her own interests, and her kids only come to her for advice they never take.

Eventually, Camille talks about leaving Zeek and she says a line that I still remember to this day—though I can't find the actual quote anywhere online. She describes how life is long and sometimes, we grow away from the people in it. They're only part of the first act, not the second. I definitely paraphrased, but that was the gist.

I agree with Camille—your life will have many acts, but that doesn't mean you'll outgrow your partner. It means you want to find a partner who will grow with you. What does that look like in a person? Someone who is open-minded to ways of thinking that aren't like theirs. A person who values learning, respecting others, and your individual growth outside of the relationship. Someone who doesn't feel the need to control and switches off between who takes the lead.

Because the fact is, every person will change throughout their life, whether they like it or not. It's only the people who fully accept growth and all the life-altering experiences that come with it that will feel like they're flowing with life, rather than swimming against it. Being open to change and new perspectives is a quality in a partner that will quite literally help your relationship last a lifetime.

KINDNESS, EVEN TOWARD STRANGERS

There's nothing more telling about a person's true character than the way they treat strangers. The person you're dating might be kind to you, but that's because they're invested in your relationship; they'll be on their best behavior with you because there's a reward. But that's not the case with strangers; they have nothing at stake. If someone's rude to people they don't know, it's a sign that they just act nice when there's some sort of gain for them.

Of course, you want your partner to be kind to you as well. Loving someone means you're showing the more vulnerable sides of yourself to another person. If they mishandle that kind of openness, you're going to feel unsafe and betrayed by them.

Kindness fosters a sense of safety within a relationship, both emotionally and physically. Being able to confide in someone and have them be gentle with your heart is crucial. It's horrible ignoring that you don't feel safe in a relationship. Doing so is a surefire way to put yourself in the path of a lot of pain. What's worse, you never know when a relationship with an unkind person can take a turn into different forms of abuse. When you're both on the same team and want to watch your relationship thrive, there's no room for mean words and tearing each other down.

RESPECT FOR BOTH YOU AND THEMSELVES

Think about the way you view and treat someone you respect: you value their opinion, prioritize their safety, and genuinely care about what they have to say. On the other hand, someone who either lost your respect or you simply don't know well enough doesn't earn much of your care or thought beyond that of an acquaintance.

When I dated Jack, the man who was eleven years older than me, he assumed the role of the "older, therefore wiser" boyfriend that I definitely never asked him to be. I could've sworn the breadcrumbs of respect he threw at me every now and then meant he valued my presence in his life, but I was very mistaken. He held my opinion with little value, stomped on my career plans whenever he got the chance, and regularly violated my boundaries emotionally and sexually. My resentment toward him filled to the brim.

In my current relationship, respect is at the forefront of every interaction. Nish never raises his voice at me. He always takes my opinion into consideration. It's never what he wants to do, it's always what we want to do; I even catch myself checking some of my behaviors because I realize I've picked up bad habits from my exes. Since our relationship consists of respect for one another, there's space where we can explore our individual identities together. There's no worry about us judging or insulting each other, yet we can joke around and not have to be serious all the time.

On the same note, when your partner has respect for themselves, they have the confidence to draw boundaries with people. They know what kind of behaviors they're willing to put up with from others and that translates into someone who isn't filled with resentment or scars from people who badly hurt them.

When you're looking for someone to be in a healthy relationship with these qualities are some of the most important to look for. They're not a guarantee you'll find the love of your life, but you can be certain that someone with these qualities is a person worth giving a shot to. Because building a thriving relationship isn't easy, but your chances are much better when you find a great person.

PART V

CREATING A LOVING RELATIONSHIP

YOU DON'T NEED GAMES IN YOUR RELATIONSHIP

||||||||||||

"If love rewarded those who played their cards right, then it wouldn't thrive off unexpected moments. The pillow talks when your guard is down. The glimpse of their smile after they did something embarrassing. The candid vulnerability; the secrets told. Love without all of the above would just be another game none of us would want to play."

By now, you've probably heard a lot of people tell you that playing games when dating is simply how you do things. Remember all that nonsense we discussed earlier about feigning a lack of interest and counting the hours and days before texting back in the early phase of dating? You may think it's harmless until you find yourself in a full-fledged relationship with someone. Then what happens to these mind games?

About a year ago, I went on a date with a guy who I knew through a group of guy friends from college. We went on a single date—lunch at a nearby cafe from my house—before I drove him to the airport, and he left for a six-week-long work trip to India. Not exactly the best way to get to know someone.

If he was a typical 20-something guy, I'm sure the course of those six weeks would've looked like the following: him sporadically texting me whenever he "got a signal." Throwing in casual flirty texts every now and then. Going a few days with no word but then sending a surprise text late at night that would spark my interest again. Or maybe, and more likely, he wouldn't have texted me at all the entire trip.

But it turned out that he wasn't the kind of person to play games. He ended up texting me every day of that trip; he didn't miss a single one. He knew he was interested in me and made his intentions clear. He flirted when appropriate, but really, we got to know a lot about each other during those six weeks. And when there were only a few days left of his trip, he made plans for us to get sushi when he returned to the United States.

That sushi date turned into many more dates and now, that man is my boyfriend, Nish, who I'm with today (you know, the one who respects me and sees me as an equal). And as I type this chapter, we'll be celebrating our one-year anniversary tomorrow; one year since I drove Nish to the airport for his six-week-long trip that could've fizzled out the connection we had on our first date.

It's clear now that things worked so perfectly because neither of us bothered to try and manipulate each other's feelings; we didn't care to keep the other guessing. But, to be honest, having such regular communication felt kind of weird at first. When you've become used to unhealthy dating habits, they feel comfortable. So much so that when you meet someone who texts you back regularly, you might get the urge to run. You'll feel like something is off when really, nothing is wrong; everything is right. You're just not used to a healthy relationship.

I'm glad I didn't run because being in a relationship where we respect each other's feelings and practice open communication ended up being the kind of healthy relationship I wanted, after years of unhealthy ones. Instead of dragging out an argument and expecting my boyfriend to guess what I'm upset about, I bring up my concerns straight away. We don't withhold our feelings from one another as a means of punishment. In fact, we don't punish each other at all. And by being vulnerable with each other (even though it's hard sometimes), we create deeper intimacy between us.

Playing mind games is like choosing a thornbush-lined path when there's a freshly mowed one right beside it. They both lead to the same destination, but when you try to manipulate your partner or vice versa, you keep choosing, again and again, the path that will hurt you and your partner most.

PEOPLE PLAY MIND GAMES OUT OF FEAR.

Love can feel like a high stakes game that you don't want to lose because if you do, it means all sorts of things like heartbreak, betrayal, and rejection. When you're put in an emotional position, your underlying fears are bound to pop up and you might project those fears onto your partner. Maybe you had your heart broken before or a parent left you when you were young. Whatever your reason is, it's not fair to your partner to assume they'll do the same. I know it's hard to see someone you're dating now as someone who's different from the people you dated in the past, but it's important to try your best to do so.

Fear is a strong emotion in any case, but even more so when you're in love. Defending yourself from pain isn't your only option, it's just one. When the impulse to ignore your partner and act like you don't care comes up, you can choose to instead talk to them about your worries. You can be honest about your fears or how your partner hurt you, rather than ignoring them. Choosing to be open with each other means you'll come to a resolution much faster than if you played games.

The relationship that feels the best will always be the one where you're happiest most often. Open and honest communication solves problems quicker and allows you both to go back to being happy again. Somewhere along the way, you may have gotten confused that a relationship needs drama and yelling and crying into a bowl of ice cream to really mean anything. But how could something that causes you so much pain possibly be the best thing for you? The answer: it can't.

A way to create more love in your relationship is to leave playing mind games out of the equation. Opt for honest communication rather than holding a grudge. Speak up about hurt feelings rather than assume your partner can read your mind. Choose what feels a little scary, because, in the long run, it's going to help maintain a healthy relationship between you and your partner. Fight the urge to play games, because they do more harm than good.

WAYS TO SHOW YOUR PARTNER RESPECT

||||||||||

"A relationship without respect is simply a match between two egos that will only result in pain and no one winning."

When you think about what makes a relationship successful, your answers would probably be similar to others: chemistry, timing, sexual attraction. Don't get me wrong: all those things are important to have. But there are a few other underrated qualities that matter, too, that don't get as much attention.

Like respect. Have you stopped to consider how important respect from your partner (or anyone for that matter) is to you? That they listen when you talk, value your opinion, and talk to you like you matter? Have you ever sat your partner down and discussed what respect means to each of you?

When I got into a relationship with my college boyfriend, Sean, it quickly turned emotionally abusive. A common theme throughout his actions—criticizing me, name-calling, dismissing my feelings—was a lack of respect. After being treated like that for over a year, I began showing Sean the same kind of contempt.

And I unknowingly carried those behaviors with me throughout my other relationships.

Then I met Nish, who exudes kindness to everyone in his life. He's the sweet person most would label as a "nice guy," but far from boring or lackluster like that stereotype suggests. All of a sudden, those habits of disrespect I picked up from my relationship with Sean were amplified because Nish never did them back to me. All this time I'd been pointing the finger at other people when really, I had fingers pointing right back at me.

Lack of respect is more likely to erode the foundation of a relationship than a lack of other qualities. It's a vicious cycle—once you feel disrespected by a partner, you start to lose respect for them as well. Then you treat them differently, because of how they treat you. And that cycle repeats, over and over.

But a lot of actions of disrespect are so small and don't seem like a big deal, that they go easily undetected. A famous relationship researcher, John Gottman, found from his decades of research that contempt is more likely to end a relationship than any other behavior. When you engage in contempt in your relationship like Sean and I did, you're essentially saying you're better than your partner; a quick path to feeling disrespected. If you're wondering what contempt looks like, it's any of the following:

- **Criticizing your partner.** This includes what you say in front of your partner and also what you say when they're not around. Disrespect doesn't always happen in person; bad-mouthing your partner when you're with other people is just as mean.

- **Name-calling.** There's never a just time to call your partner an "idiot" or "jerk." There's no positive outcome that results from name-calling; all it achieves is making your partner feel distanced from you.

- **Mocking your partner.** People mock others when they want that person to feel stupid. Belittling is an unkind thing to do and will only make your partner become defensive.

- **Your body language.** This looks like rolling your eyes, crossing your arms, and refusing to look at your partner. They're simple gestures but ones that create a barrier for being open with each other.

The bright side of all of this is there are easy ways to show your partner respect. Aside from cutting out the above, try changing your behavior in these ways:

ACCEPT THAT YOU BOTH HAVE DIFFERENT OPINIONS AND WAYS OF DOING THINGS

Sean berated me over my smallest actions: how I cleaned the bathroom meant I was "careless," the way I ate made me a "slob," and my political beliefs were "uneducated". He had no respect for the fact I wasn't just like him. If your goal in a relationship is to find someone you never disagree with, you're going to be on that journey for the rest of your life.

No two people share the exact same views and opinions, but that's not a bad thing. Being with someone who has opinions different from yours means you have a chance to widen your perspective and learn a bit about acceptance. Instead of trying to make your partner see things your way, respect that you both think of the world differently, and see the beauty in that fact. Ask them to explain the way they see things so you can better understand who they are. Focus on accepting your partner, rather than trying to change them.

PRACTICE TRUST

Respecting someone includes trusting them until they give you a reason not to.

But I know this can be hard for people, especially when your trust has been broken in the past.

When I first started dating my boyfriend, Nish, I had a hard time trusting him. After Sean threatened to leave me and Patrick cheated on me, I was terrified it would happen again.

If trusting doesn't come easily for you, then you have to build it up. Sit your partner down and have a conversation about your experience with trust and how it affects you today. Keep track of the moments when your partner is there for you and gives you reasons to believe their sincerity. Consider the beliefs you have about trusting romantic partners, where they came from, and consider how they hold up in terms of your current relationship.

LISTEN TO WHAT THEY SAY

Actively listening to your partner is more than just the everyday listening you do when your neighbor stops you on the sidewalk to tell you about their day. It involves actually hearing and understanding what your partner is saying. When you actively listen, you're telling your partner, "I care about what you're telling me. I'm here for you."

All too often, people are caught up in what they'll say next that they don't actually hear what the point the other person is trying to convey. You might overstep their words or completely miss the point. But actively listening strengthens relationships. Next time your partner wants to talk about something serious, sit down with them. Put away your phone. Make eye contact as they speak to you. Focus on exactly what they're saying and ask questions if something is confusing. You can also try repeating back to them what you heard, in an effort to really understand one another.

VALIDATE YOUR PARTNER'S FEELINGS

Don't dismiss your partner's feelings as "irrational" or "dramatic." What someone feels is what they feel, whether or not you agree. The fact is, when your partner is upset, they're upset. And you telling them not to be isn't going to help.

In a relationship, it's important that both partners feel comfortable speaking up about what they're struggling with without fear of judgment from the other person. This creates a deep sense of trust; something the best couples have an abundance of. Statements like, "I can see you're upset" or "I understand why you're mad" go a long way. When you validate your partner's feelings, rather than dismissing them, you're entering their world. You stay with your partner in that vulnerable moment and try to understand things from their perspective.

TALKING ABOUT YOUR PAST WITH SOMEONE NEW

||||||||||

"When the time comes, don't be scared that you'll say too much or show too many feelings. The right person will meet you with gentleness; they'll be kind with your vulnerability because they'll understand that those tender parts of your past created the person they love today."

There's no rulebook for what you have to share with your partner about your past. You can be as open as you want or choose to forget some memories. This makes me think about the debate on whether or not to share your sexual history with your partner. Do you tell them how many people you slept with or do you keep it to yourself? The answer: do whatever makes you feel comfortable. I know my boyfriend's sexual history, simply because I asked, and he felt comfortable sharing. But he doesn't know about mine, because he doesn't want to. It's that simple.

But that's only one (arguably, small) part of your past. What I care more about is the parts of your past you want to share, but are scared to. The kind that feels very personal to you, but were traumatic or shaped you in such a significant way, they still affect you today.

I always felt this way about my depression. I experienced it throughout middle school and in college. I still struggle with it to this day. My worst bouts of depression consumed my life to the point that both the disease and the recovery deeply altered who I am forever. While I now see those experiences as a process that helped me understand myself better, sharing that part of my life with Nish felt scary. For a long time, I felt like a puzzle; composed of all these broken pieces that I wanted to put out on a table and have my partner put back together.

But talking to your partner about your past shouldn't feel like you're a bad person or broken. The fact is, everyone has been through pain in some way. We're all a little scarred, but our scars are what shaped us into the thoughtful, reflective people we are today. Without your past, you'd be a different person; perhaps someone your partner wouldn't want to be with.

Talking about your past is a choice only you can make. Maybe your wounds feel too fresh and you want to process them on your own for a bit longer. Or perhaps your stories are waiting, just beneath your surface, to be told to someone you deeply love. If you are ready to talk about your past with your partner, then there are a few things you should keep in mind.

DETERMINE WHETHER YOU FEEL ENOUGH TRUST WITH THEM

It's important you feel safe enough in your relationship to not only share your experiences but that you feel your partner will honor your feelings about your past, rather than dismiss them. Vulnerability with some of your most painful memories isn't something to do lightly; if your partner isn't able to meet you in a mature, emotional space, you may be left feeling disappointed by their reaction. A good way to determine if they could handle this conversation is by reflecting on how they handled serious talks, confrontations, or emotional scenarios before.

REMEMBER THAT YOU'RE NOT BROKEN

When you decide the time is right and you want to open up to your partner, don't go into the conversation feeling like you're broken or a bad person. You're a human being with a past, just like everyone else. You aren't broken and you're still worthy of love. Don't speak from a place of shame. Convey your past with honesty, truth, and a bit of courage.

LET YOUR PARTNER KNOW YOU HAVE SOMETHING IMPORTANT TO TALK ABOUT

Jumping straight into a serious conversation can be a bit jarring for someone if they don't see it coming. Give your partner a bit of a heads up, so they can mentally prepare. The last thing you want is for them to be checking their phone or suddenly jump up to answer the door for the take-out they ordered. The same goes for when they're trying to fall asleep or just woke up. Set the tone, and their expectations. Pick a time where you're both alert and present.

TALK WHEN YOU'RE BOTH UNDISTRACTED

Choose a time when you're both free of distractions; don't choose the middle of a movie or when they're playing video games to suddenly spring the conversation on them. Talking about something as important as this means you deserve a time slot when neither of you are busy. If that means asking them to talk later that day, then so be it.

LET YOUR PARTNER KNOW YOU DON'T NEED THEM TO FIX YOU

It's a sweet, yet oftentimes burdensome, truth that our partners hear our painful stories and automatically want to help, even if the pain happened years ago. It doesn't make sense to everyone that sometimes, you just want to share a story and don't need a solution. Tell your partner that while you love how they care enough to help, you don't need them to fix anything; you just want to share part of your past that shaped who you are today.

ASK IF THEY HAVE ANY QUESTIONS OR WANT TO SHARE THEIR STRUGGLES

Sometimes, we relay stories in a confusing way or bring up a subject the other person has no experience with. When you're nearly done talking about your story, see if your partner has any questions; open up the floor for them to better understand exactly what you went through. After that, ask if they want to share anything about their past; maybe your decision to be vulnerable will inspire them to do the same. If they're not ready, let them know you'd love to listen when they are.

THE DOS AND DON'TS OF ARGUING

||||||||||

"The words you let carelessly roll off your tongue carry well past the heated moment you said them in."

We all communicate every single day. It's not just in the words we say, but how we say them, our body language, and how we listen. For something we do every day, you'd think people would be great at communicating. It might come as a surprise to you that arguing (which boils down to poor communication skills) is the main problem people have when they reach out to me for relationship advice. I've heard everything from, "my partner won't get off their phone" to "I never feel understood" to "I feel like our fights are going to end our relationship."

It's not fun hearing this from people about a skill that isn't that hard to learn but to be fair, I was once in their shoes. I've watched countless arguments turn into screaming fights. I've barely been able to stay awake in classes because of how emotionally drained I felt after a fight. And while I could sit here and talk about all the things my exes did wrong in arguments, and I will below, I can't ignore that I also had my faults, too. Sometimes it's a tough pill to swallow that we're not perfect, but doing so allows us to make changes that help us grow and become better partners.

During arguments with Sean, I'd call him names as a way to defend myself against the awful things he said to me. I would cry with Patrick and Alex to try and make them understand how hurt I was. And with Jack, I'd be passive-aggressive with my tactics, often ignoring him if he did something to upset me.

While I'm not proud to admit that, I also don't fault my younger self. I picked up those habits from childhood, interacting with my parents, and the ghosts of my relationship past. And the fact is, I can't go back and change what's already happened and the ways I acted. But what I can do is look out for those nasty ways of fighting and challenge myself to do better.

I mentioned this before, but becoming a couple with Nish opened my eyes to how a healthy relationship functions. Staying level-headed during an argument comes naturally for him and by being with someone who has never raised his voice at me or called me a name, I couldn't help but notice my own actions. His patience contrasted with my impatience. His level-headed thinking clashed with my emotion-filled fears. Don't get me wrong, he never made me feel bad for my actions; but when you're the only person snapping for no reason, you quickly stop doing it.

As much as I didn't want to admit that I needed to work on my own communication skills, doing so helped our relationship. And learning how to argue better helps me maintain my sense of peace and happiness, regardless if Nish and I have a disagreement. It's a win-win all around.

I'm not adding this essay to help you stop all your arguments. Far from, actually. While arguing doesn't necessarily feel good, numerous studies show that they're healthy for relationships. Couples who argue hash out issues rather than bottling them up. They learn more about each other and create healthy compromises. But most importantly, they care enough about the relationship to have conversations that are uncomfortable.

Let that fact assure you if you argue in your relationship, it's a good sign. There are respectful ways to argue with your partner that make you both feel safe and understood. But there are also ways to argue that will make you both want to rip out your hair and could ultimately hurt your relationship. My guess is you want to avoid the latter and have your arguments feel like the former. If so, then let's talk about the do's and don'ts of arguing that make for a smoother relationship.

DO FOCUS ON ONE ISSUE AT A TIME
DON'T BRING UP PAST MISTAKES AS AMMO

Once the vibe has been set for an argument, it might be tempting to bring up everything you have an issue with since you're already upset. But think of it this way: if multiple things in your apartment are broken, you don't try to fix everything at once. You're only a single person; you have to focus on one project before moving onto the next. The same goes for an argument, you want to give your full attention to one issue without veering off into other ones.

Focus on the facts, feelings, and the present. Don't bring up your partner's mistakes they made two months ago that you already talked about because you think it better supports your argument now. That's not fair to them or the change they might be trying to make. Focus on what's happening in your relationship today since the past is already over.

DO SHOW YOUR PARTNER RESPECT
DON'T NAME-CALL

Nothing felt more demoralizing in arguments with Sean than when he called me a jerk, dumb or fat. Coming from someone who should've been on my team, his words stung to the point that I'd start calling him names as a way to not feel the pain he caused me. And both of the words we both carelessly spewed were ones we couldn't take back. Someone might be able to forgive what you say, but they'll forever have been said.

Engaging in name-calling is a prime example of disrespect. Just like you'd never call your best friend, role model, or grandmother a rude name, there's never a reason to do the same to your partner. All it does is aim to hurt them; arguing is about coming to an understanding, not causing pain to the other person.

DO FOCUS ON YOUR FEELINGS
DON'T PLAY THE BLAME-GAME

The way you talk to your partner can mean the difference between them being open to understanding you and feeling like they need to defend themselves. Once your partner feels like they're being attacked, it's hard to come to a solution.

Instead, focus on your emotions; while you both might've seen a situation from different perspectives, no one can argue that you didn't feel a certain way. Instead of stating that your partner doesn't put in as much work as you do into the relationship, you might want to say something like, "I feel alone in the relationship sometimes. I want my effort to be reciprocated by you." On the same hand, they'll feel less like you're being blamed if you can try to see things from their perspective. "I know things don't come naturally to you and that you need time to work on getting better," could go a long way.

DO TAKE A BREAK WHEN YOU NEED ONE
DON'T STONEWALL

There's nothing wrong with needing time to collect yourself, breathe, and think about things. But if you don't voice that need to your partner, it's unfair to them. When you suddenly walk away from your partner and ignore them, it's disrespectful and confusing to them.

If you know you're the type of person who needs to cool down, simply say to your partner, "I'm feeling very upset about this argument. Can we revisit this conversation later today at dinner?" That way you've voiced what you're experiencing and acknowledged you'll talk about things at another time.

DO REMEMBER YOU'RE A TEAM
DON'T FOCUS ON "WINNING"

The moment you start thinking of you and your partner as a team is when you'll change your arguing game for the best. Teammates work towards the same goal. They have the relationship's best interest in mind and want to come to a solution that works for everyone.

But the moment you start thinking it's you against your partner, things become ugly. You'll lose sight of why you're arguing and do whatever it takes to win. You might do things I mentioned above, like blame your partner for everything or call them names. That distance will grow and grow between you two until you realize you're in a terrible fight.

So instead, remind yourself you're on the same team. Better yet, state it out loud. Let your partner know how much you value coming to a fix to whatever the issue is in which you both feel understood and have a solid plan to move forward.

DO ACTIVELY LISTEN
DON'T INTERRUPT YOUR PARTNER

Most of the time, couples argue more than they need to because they don't understand one another. One person takes something the other says the wrong way and vice versa. They interrupt each other because they're too focused on trying to get their point across. Not to mention they completely miss what their partner said because they're in their head crafting a comeback. But none of that is good communication.

Instead, practice active listening by paying attention to what your partner tells you. Once they're done speaking, summarize what they just said back to them so you can make sure you understand what they meant. If you have questions, ask them. Then it's your turn to talk.

By actively listening to each other, you slow down the conversation and give each point the attention they deserve, making the argument a lot shorter and hurtful than it would've been.

DO EXPLAIN HOW YOU FELT AND HUG IT OUT
DON'T IGNORE EACH OTHER

What you do after an argument is just as important as what you do during. You can either ignore one another and let resentment hang in the air, or you can hug it out and come back to a happy place sooner.

Of course, I don't expect you to force emotions that aren't there or bottle up any pent-up feelings you have. Take all the time you need to collect yourself but, when you're ready, reconnect with your partner, apologize if necessary, and come up with a plan for a better future. If things got a little out of hand, figure out how you can both do better next time.

TRUSTING YOUR PARTNER WHEN IT FEELS TOO HARD

||||||||||

"The way you show up for your present love is shaped by the way you experienced love in the past."

I know the go-to advice is to "trust someone until they give you a reason not to," but what if trusting a new person doesn't come easily? What about those of us whose trust has been betrayed by the people we loved? Logic doesn't prevail, especially when someone's been through a painful experience. I mentioned building trust earlier, but I really want to explore this topic because of how greatly it affected my love life and how it can help you in the future.

When I first started dating my boyfriend, Nish, I couldn't give him my full trust; I could barely shell out half-trust. I was skeptical of how kind he was and scared to fully open up to his love.

And that's not because of the type of person Nish is or anything he did; it's because of what I've been through with boyfriends in the past. The pain I've felt from my ex cheating on me and Sean being verbally abusive left me feeling like all men would eventually hurt me. I couldn't help but think, "Would Nish be just like the rest of them?"

But I knew I couldn't give in to that way of thinking; trust is a key part of any relationship. And even in my new one, I heard the slight irritation in my boyfriend's voice when I questioned, for the fifth time, why he was so nice to me; when I pointed my finger and said, "What's your angle?"—a kidding tone covering up my very serious question.

Trust is expected to be given easily but it's different for those of us who have scars from their past. It's a sad reality, but when you've been hurt, a new partner will have to take on the task of proving you can trust them, no matter how much you want to inherently give that trust. But just as much, if not more, you must take on the task of learning how to trust again.

Trust is a decision, like any other change you make, that only you can commit to. It's not easy work, but it's a choice that'll bring you happiness and peace in your relationship. So, let's talk about how you get there. How do you trust someone when it feels impossible?

BEGIN BY ACCEPTING YOU'RE NOT ALONE IF YOU FIND IT HARD TO TRUST PEOPLE

If you find it hard to trust your partner, it's because you've experienced betrayal: the first time someone promised they'd love you forever and then changed their mind, a lover who swore themselves only to you but went ahead and cheated anyway. Whatever your experience looked like, that pain is real.

It embeds itself in the very essence of who you are. The pages of your manual for how love works are filled with your experiences, but luckily, you have a chance to write new pages and learn from the old.

YOUR PAIN IS NOT BAGGAGE; IT'S LESSONS

I want you to let go of the idea you're "broken." Quit thinking you're undateable, that you come with some kind of burden dragged behind you. Every person has their own pain that shaped who they are today. But what defines you as a person is how you move forward with that pain.

The betrayal of a lover can either weigh you down or help you identify your values. Choosing the latter assists boundaries and effectively communicating your expectations for your relationship moving forward.

RECOGNIZE PATTERNS IN YOUR PAST RELATIONSHIPS

If you're worried about being duped in a new relationship, identify the common themes from your exes. Were they constantly belittling you? Did they jump in quickly with a lot of emotions and then later withdraw?

Often, people seek what's familiar to them. If you're not careful, you could get into new relationships that are just like your past ones. Maybe because you feel like loose ends aren't tied up from your past relationships; you want a happy ending you never got. But recognizing red flags from your past will help you identify them in current partners. If you begin dating someone with those same characteristics as your exes that hurt you, then you can stop yourself before things go too far.

TAKE THINGS AT A SLOW PACE

If you're wary of new partners, take things slowly. Get a good feel for whether or not you think the person is worthy of trust. Ask your friends and family for their opinion on the person if you're hesitant. You'd be surprised how well they can judge a person's intentions since they see things from an objective standpoint. Trust your instincts, or those closest to you, if things don't feel right.

When I first dated my boyfriend, I implemented a new process of dating, where I checked in with myself regularly. I shifted my thinking from worrying if he wanted to date me to deciding if he was someone I wanted to spend my time with. I went at my own pace, even though I knew my boyfriend for years before we first decided to make things romantic. But that choice allowed me to feel more at ease with the relationship; I never felt in over my head.

LOOK AT THINGS FROM A DATA STANDPOINT

It's hard not to get caught up in the great feelings that come with a blossoming relationship; I understand because I was addicted to all those feelings when it came to love. But if you feel like those emotions might be clouding your judgment, look at the hard facts you do have.

What kind of person are they? Do they lie to their friends? Are they close to their family? Have they cheated in the past (that you know of)? How is their relationship with their mom/sisters? Do they seem like a genuinely good person?

The answers to these questions will end up being more telling than any "butterflies" you instinctively have.

COMMUNICATE HOW YOU'RE FEELING

People are too conservative when it comes to talking about their past. If you're having difficulty trusting your partner, maybe it's time to have a conversation with them about why you're experiencing these feelings. An understanding between partners makes for a beautiful relationship; you explain why you have some peculiar behaviors and why certain actions trigger you.

Deciding to date someone isn't only about committing to who you see in the present, it's committing to their past as well. Your past loves shape your current love. An open conversation about why you find it hard to trust could clear the air for your partner.

TRUST YOU CAN MAKE BETTER DECISIONS

It may be hard to trust other people, but sometimes it's even harder to admit that you can't trust yourself. I still struggle with this concept. Thinking about my past and how I was abused, both sexually and emotionally, makes me upset. I think, "How did I let myself be used the way I did? Why didn't I stand up for myself?"

That kind of regret isn't helpful to me. I know what the red flags are to avoid the type of men I used to date. All I can do is trust that I'll be more vigilant this time. All I can do is forgive myself for my less-than-stellar decisions in the past. Checking in with yourself and going back to your values and boundaries will help you feel more secure in the decisions you make today.

WORK WITH A PROFESSIONAL

If your past feels too difficult to move through on your own, consider seeing a therapist or counselor. About three years ago, I started seeing a new therapist with the sole purpose of figuring out why I dated men who mistreated me. It took a lot of talking, a lot of dredging up painful memories, but I came to so many beautiful realizations.

Therapy is excellent in that it helps you realize how your past affects you today. A therapist can also give you tools and develop strategies for you to form healthy, new relationships moving forward. Plus, nowadays, there are affordable means for finding professional help, whether that be online or at a community center near you.

Because it's natural to want to protect your heart when it's been broken in the past, it's scary to trust a new person again; I know, I've been there too. But while it's scary to be vulnerable again, I think it's scarier to lose out on something amazing because you guarded your heart too diligently. There's always a chance you'll be hurt again, but know you'll be okay if that does happen.

On the brighter side, there's a chance you'll find a love that would never purposely try to cause you pain, who has your best interests in mind. But it all begins with a decision to learn to trust again that only you can make.

WHY INVESTING IN YOURSELF WILL BENEFIT YOUR RELATIONSHIP

||||||||||

"You can't hand your happiness and growth over to someone else; those are lifetime investments that only you can make. Other people can support and encourage you along the way, but the work must be done by you."

I remember the night Nish officially asked me to be his girlfriend. I don't subscribe to the notion that a woman has to wait around for a man to make this move, but I wasn't in a rush. I knew where the relationship was going. And though I was excited he finally worked up the courage to ask me, I started worrying during the drive home.

Earlier that day, I went over to my not-yet-boyfriend's apartment to grab handrolls at a nearby Japanese restaurant. I'm a sucker for a great lobster roll, so I was thoroughly enjoying our rather regular date. We walked back to his place and watched several episodes of *The Good Place* because it's forking great (if you've seen it, you'll understand).

I had to wake up early for work the next day so when it got to be around midnight, I decided to go home. Nish and I walked down to my car in the parking garage and started to say our typical goodbyes. But this time, he seemed nervous. His eyes were looking around and he kept trying to say something but was getting lost in recollecting on how us dating had gone so far.

I'm no newbie to this. I knew what he was about to ask me. I stood there until he was finally able to say the words.

"Do you want to be my girlfriend," Nish asked.

"Of course I do," I replied.

And the rest was history.

Well, that is, until I got in the car and a bit of panic ensued. I'd spent the year before dating Nish building a life I loved. One where I didn't have to make decisions based on another person. One where I could binge-watch *The Good Place* all on my own for two days in a row if I forking wanted to.

I worried about how my life would change now that I had a man who seriously wanted to date me. I knew this guy wasn't going to be a man I casually dated; he'd always been the type of person who knew he wanted a relationship. A healthy and happy one, but a relationship nonetheless.

My mixture of excitement and worry was present within me for weeks to follow. I brought up my thoughts about this to one of my friends, and she told me about how she went through the same thing. She said that people talk about getting into a relationship like it will rock your world in the best way possible and, while everyone hopes that's the case, it still rocks your world. Your life goes through a significant period of change. Just like anything, it takes a bit of time to adjust.

If taking a year off from dating taught me anything, it was that I needed to have a lot of awareness while I adjusted to my new relationship. I'd written on healthy relationships and read enough books to know that the best relationships are the ones where each person in the relationship maintains their self-identity. While I didn't want to feel this worry after getting into a relationship that felt so right and healthy, I saw how I could use it to my advantage.

In my relationships before, I let myself become consumed by my partner's life. I mean, look at how things went with my college boyfriend, Sean. He literally moved in with me right when we started dating and managed to cut me off from my friends soon after. If that's not unhealthily enmeshing our lives, I don't know what is.

With Sean, I became an emotionally reliant shell of the person I used to be. I didn't prioritize or even balance my life outside of him and that ended with me feeling too attached to a man who treated me like crap and feeling lost when our relationship ended. I knew my relationship with Nish needed to be different.

ONE PIECE OF ADVICE I HEARD ALONG MY JOURNEY IN BETTER UNDERSTANDING LOVE IS THAT YOUR HAPPINESS IS SOMETHING ONLY YOU CAN CREATE.

If you expect another person to do it for you, you'll be continuously disappointed, not to mention that it's wholly unfair to the other person.

That's why making sure you invest energy and time into your life outside of your relationship is vital to the success of your relationship itself. It might sound counterintuitive that spending time elsewhere benefits another aspect of your life, but think of it this way:

When do you feel most fulfilled with life? Is it when you focus all your energy on one aspect like work or school? Or is it when you see your friends, take care of yourself, drink enough water, work toward your goals, and see your family?

I'm assuming you chose the latter.

So now the question is, which version of yourself do you believe makes for the best partner? Your most fulfilled self? Or one where you're drained and neglecting parts of your life that mean a lot to you?

Again, it's a no-brainer. We show up as our best selves for the relationship (and this applies to friendships and family as well) when we are our best selves.

Now that I'm a little over a year into my relationship with Nish, I'm happy to say that maintaining my identity outside of the relationship (and him the same) has done wonders for our love. We both balance our hobbies and seeing friends and family with the time we spend together.

Now comes the part where I fill you in on how I did this, so you can do the same.

WRITE DOWN WHAT YOUR PRIORITIES ARE

Sometimes, people don't really know what their priorities are—they just default to what everyone else says: friends, family, work, and health. But when I first got into my current relationship, I wrote out my specific priorities on a piece of paper. I had several friends whose friendships I wanted to keep strong. My writing career meant the world to me. I loved reading and wanted time to do that. And, to be frank, those were my top three priorities.

By becoming clear on what I valued most in my life, I could ensure I made time for them. Instead of being vague on what mattered, I pinpointed exactly what I needed to focus on to maintain my self-identity.

Writing your priorities down will not only help you determine what they are, but they'll also feel even more important just by having them physically exist.

FIGURE OUT YOUR LONG-TERM GOALS

Once you know your priorities, it's time to think about what your long-term goals are surrounding them. For me, my writing career was new and needed a lot of attention. Most of my long-term goals are focused on my career, since I love the work I do.

By acknowledging where I wanted to go with my writing, I could be realistic about the time I needed to spend putting pen to paper. I couldn't sleepover at my boyfriend's place, wake up at noon, grab lunch, and not get home until 2 pm. My best writing is done in the mornings, and that meant that a lot of nights, I opted to sleep at my own place.

HAVE AN OPEN CONVERSATION WITH YOUR PARTNER

If you're a worrier like me, you might feel like asserting that you want alone time or to hang out with your friends will come off like you don't care about the relationship. While that's far from the truth and a whole other can of worms, I've found that honesty is your best bet for alleviating these thoughts.

For me, I sat my boyfriend down during the beginning of our relationship and created an understanding with him (I hate using the word rule because it sounds so formal). During the weekdays, I needed to leave his house by 11 pm so I could get home, sleep, and write in the morning. He understood and helped me stick to that curfew (though I broke it a couple of times on my own accord).

No matter how new the relationship is, it's going to benefit you both to create an honest channel of communication. A few conversation starters you can use are:

"I noticed I haven't been feeling right lately and a night to myself to take a bath and watch TV is what I need right now."

"I want to balance our relationship with seeing my friends, and for you to do the same. Let's set aside time to see them every week."

"Let's both take some 'me time' tonight since we've had stressful weeks. We can have a date night tomorrow."

BEGIN A NEW HOBBY

If you have a hobby that you love like crazy and takes up a lot of your time, skip this section. If you're like me and have vague ideas of hobbies you like, then keep reading.

Nothing says, "I'm prioritizing my happiness" like starting an entirely new hobby. You'll not only need to put a significant amount of time in to learn it, but you'll feel extremely proud for accomplishing something new.

Like many people in Los Angeles, I became obsessed with house plants after buying one at a farmer's market. My new green purchase was around the same time I started dating Nish. And, like many people in L.A. I quickly realized that plants require a lot more work than just watering them every now and then. Some need special soil, while others need a specific amount of lighting.

Learning all about plants, soil, pots, and watering was not only fun but fulfilling. I mean, I've grown plants from mere sprouts. Creating a thriving pothos plant from a cutting is a surefire way to make you a proud plant mom—or whatever your newfound hobby is.

TALK TO OR SEE A FRIEND, AT LEAST ONCE A WEEK

I can't stress enough how important it is to have connections with people outside of your relationship. Intimacy doesn't have to happen only with your partner. Platonic intimacy is just as important to have in your life, especially if you lean towards emotionally depending on your relationship.

Pick up the phone for a talk or plan a dinner date with one of your friends, at least once a week. No matter how busy you are, find the time to catch up with someone even if it's only for thirty minutes. You'll never regret a call with someone who's important to you.

Luckily, I have a best friend who calls me at least twice a week, even when it sometimes annoys me. I love her to death, though, and am grateful she is religious about calling me. Even if we can only spare twenty minutes to talk, I leave our conversations with a sense of fullness that only my friends can bring into my life.

CREATE WHATEVER BOUNDARIES ARE NECESSARY

Like I stated above, a boundary I quickly created early on in my relationship was prioritizing my writing. Even today, my boyfriend and I plan events like seeing his family around my writing schedule. Since I'm a freelance writer, I have to organize my own schedule since I don't have a boss making sure I stay on track.

Depending on your priorities and goals you came up with, you'll want to create boundaries with your partner to ensure you can allocate time to them. If you have an on-going Thursday night dinner planned with your best friend, then let your partner know you're busy those nights. Someone who respects and cares for your well-being will understand that boundaries are good for a relationship. They might have questions or try to compromise with you, but they won't try to pressure you into letting go of your boundaries completely.

CHECK IN WITH HOW YOU'RE FEELING

The most important part of maintaining your sense of self in a relationship is being aware of how you're feeling. You can't stand up for your needs, create boundaries, and grow as an individual if you aren't in touch with your emotions.

All too often, I ignored my feelings in favor of making my partner happy. I sometimes believed the sadness I felt could be fixed through my boyfriends. But if I'd asked myself if my needs were being met and put words to the emotions I experienced, I would've realized that I missed seeing my friends or felt unfulfilled with how my life was turning out.

Taking inventory of your emotions and knowing what to do to self-regulate (aka soothe yourself when you're stressed out, like calling a friend) will strengthen your sense of autonomy. You won't need your partner to make you feel better. This is important because, sometimes, they'll have their own emotions to manage but you'll be equipped with knowledge of how to take care of yourself, without needing someone else.

HEALTHY VS. UNHEALTHY COMPROMISE

||||||||||

"In love, you won't think the same, you won't do chores the same, you won't eat foods that are the same, and you won't spend your free time the same. But love isn't about trying to work together to be the same; it's about existing with a person who is entirely their own person and learning to be together in ways you're both happy."

A client once assigned me an article about revamping people's dating profiles. It had been a while since I'd swiped on apps, so I downloaded the three major ones. After looking over the sections in each dating profile, I had a brilliant idea.

Instead of deleting the apps, I'd interview real-life daters, AKA my matches. I created a typical dating profile but instead filled out my bio to say that I wasn't looking to date but that I'm a writer who wants to interview people about their dating lives. Surprisingly, a lot of people were down to talk.

I asked them all kinds of questions from how their dating life was going to what their biggest dating fears are. One person whose response interested me was a guy we'll call Blake. Blake's profile told me a few things about him: he's a 29-year old brunette who has long hair, loves to snowboard, and enjoys a good taco. We got to chatting and it turned out that he's never been in a serious relationship. I asked if he wanted one, and Blake replied that he did but with one significant caveat.

"I love being able to do whatever I want when I want," Blake said, "I can wake up and decide to go surfing one morning and then go away to the mountains for a weekend. I'm scared that a relationship will take away from my true love: being outdoors."

I couldn't help but feel like Blake was unknowingly onto something here. It's completely reasonable to be afraid of losing something you love in exchange for something else. But does that mean Blake has to forgo love and essentially marry his longboard?

I wasn't on those apps to give advice, but Blake asked what I thought of his predicament. My thoughts were simple.

"I think you're focusing a lot on what you'll lose instead of what you'll gain," I replied.

What Blake struggled with was the idea of compromise. He believed that to have a girlfriend, he would need to give up his passions. But he also thought that being in a relationship meant those two loves couldn't be blended.

Compromise has always been an interesting topic for me. The age-old advice is to tell people, "relationships are about compromise," but that's extremely vague. What kind of compromise is good and which compromises are bad?

When I dated Sean, my college boyfriend, I thought compromise meant creating all of our plans around his acting schedule. I thought it looked like me working out with him four times a week, instead of hanging out with my friends. I believed compromise was me giving up parts of my life for Sean's. I never realized all of this "compromising" severely favored his interests.

It's true that relationships consist of coming to agreements. Getting into a romantic relationship with another human being is complicated. You both have your own thoughts, beliefs, backgrounds, and past experiences. Merging those into one cohesive relationship comes with some work.

But while a relationship is about understanding and sometimes giving instead of getting, there are a lot of situations where people get into relationships where they give up too much of their life. That's why it's important to understand the signs of whether your compromises are healthy or unhealthy.

HEALTHY COMPROMISE IS BALANCED UNHEALTHY COMPROMISE FAVORS ONE PARTNER

When you're in a relationship, both you and your partner deserve to have your needs met. Say, for instance, the topic of your friends comes up. I'm sure both of you want to spend time hanging out with the people most important to you. Sometimes, you probably want your partner there, too.

Balancing seeing your friends and theirs is a healthy compromise. But if your partner only wants to see their friends and you feel like it's been ages since he hung out with yours, that's unhealthy.

When there's a situation where both of your needs can't be met at once, you meet in the middle. Having to completely forego what you want isn't fair to you.

HEALTHY COMPROMISE LEADS TO GROWTH UNHEALTHY COMPROMISE LEADS TO RESENTMENT

Again, if you sacrifice too much for the relationship while your partner sacrifices next to nothing, you'll come to resent them. This includes a small decision like choosing where to eat to bigger life decisions such as marriage. If your opinions feel like they have very little weight when it comes to making choices, you won't feel respected. While compromise will always lead to giving up a little of what you want, the healthy kind will lead to the growth of the relationship.

HEALTHY COMPROMISE MAKES YOU FEEL SAFE UNHEALTHY COMPROMISE MAKES YOU FEEL UNSAFE

When you healthily compromise, you feel emotionally and physically safe with any decisions made. But unhealthy compromise is the exact opposite. Sean once threatened to leave me unless I'd have a threesome with him and another girl (I know, horrible). I was so scared of the thought of losing him, I began to convince myself that I could go through with it. But I never did, and I'm glad I didn't sacrifice my emotional safety for a guy. Sean trying to coerce me into bringing another woman into our bed was a very unhealthy form of compromise.

HEALTHY COMPROMISE FEELS ALIGNED WITH YOUR AUTHENTIC SELF UNHEALTHY COMPROMISE FEELS LIKE THE OPPOSITE

Though you won't completely get your way, compromise should still feel like it's in alignment with your values and morals. It can't completely cross your boundaries or leave you feeling like you don't know who you are anymore. Take Blake for example. He wanted his adventurous lifestyle to stay intact but also craved a relationship. Healthy compromise would be finding someone who loved to surf and snowboard with him. Unhealthy compromise would look like him giving up his passions for his partner. And my guess is that he could only envision the latter.

QUESTIONS TO ASK YOUR PARTNER TO UNDERSTAND THEM ON A DEEPER LEVEL

||||||||||

"Part of loving is being able to show the sides of you that most people never see—the weird, the not-so-pretty, the damaged bits—and having the other person love you even more."

Since you're reading this book, you're most likely someone who not only values love and connection with people, but you want to strengthen both of them. You're not the type to let relationships just happen to you; playing an active role is more your style. And while dinner dates, visiting a museum, and movie nights are fun and important to a great relationship, you might get to a point where you want to get to know someone a little deeper.

I've always been that kind of person, too. I thrive off late-night pillow talk and sharing my feelings at the moment. It's always been an easier endeavor with romantic partners, but I work on doing the same with other relationships in my life. I'll be honest; these conversations haven't always gone well. My college boyfriend, Sean, hated talking about feelings and would threaten to leave me once he realized how scared I was that he'd abandon me. But I chalk that up to my 21-year-old self being a bad judge in character when it came to who I shared my intimate feelings with. Because when it comes to Nish, we've had plenty of talks about our fears, hopes for the future, and our past. The results have been that both of us feel closer to each other. Neither of us would dream of using what we discovered as ammo for future arguments. And again, this just goes to show how finding a genuinely good person (and not ignoring those red flags) is important when looking for a relationship. Those experiences with Nish, and positive ones with other boyfriends, help me stand firm on the fact that certain questions can benefit your relationships and help you connect in ways you and your partner normally wouldn't.

Before you jump into the questions, it's important to first set the mood. If your partner comes home after a tough workout at the gym and you bombard them with, "Tell me about your deepest childhood trauma," chances are they won't have the best answer for you. So, while it's tempting to bring up questions when they pop into your head (or once you read them below), you need to allow your partner space to mentally prepare and choose a time that works for them as well. That way, both of you are in the best position for digging deeper.

And while we're at it, remember that whatever questions you ask your partner is fair game for them to ask back to you. If it isn't something you would feel comfortable answering, you may want to hold off on asking it. But at the same time, remember that these questions aren't tests. They're opportunities for both of you to strengthen what you already have. There are no wrong answers, but these questions do involve a little courage, honesty, and the ability to laugh at yourself. They'll fluctuate between light and deeper subjects. Think of these questions as a sort of fun activity; a game where there's you're both winners.

QUESTIONS ABOUT LIFE

- What are your must-do's in life on your bucket list?
- When you were a kid, what did you want to be when you grew up?
- What do you look forward to when you wake up each day?
- What was your favorite vacation you ever took and why?
- Is there anything you would change about yourself?
- If you could easily change jobs, would you? If so, which career would you choose?
- If you woke up tomorrow with no fear, what would you do first?
- If you could write a note to your younger self, what would you say in only three sentences?
- When was the last time you cried?
- When was the last time you laughed so hard your stomach hurt?

QUESTIONS ABOUT THEIR FAVORITES

- What's your favorite movie?
- Favorite book?
- Favorite kind of food?
- What's your favorite childhood memory?
- What was your favorite subject in school?
- Did you have a favorite teacher?
- What's your favorite thing about yourself?

QUESTIONS ABOUT YOUR RELATIONSHIP

- What's something you want to do together one day?

- What do you see happening for us in the next year, as a couple?

- What's your favorite memory with me?

- Were there any moments when I let you down?

- What did you first think of me when we met?

- What's your favorite non-physical quality about me?

- What do I do that makes you feel most loved?

- What ways do you like to show your love? (Words, touch, gifts, helping, quality time)

- What's one secret you haven't told me yet?

QUESTIONS ABOUT NOTHING AND EVERYTHING

- If you won a million dollars, what's the first thing you would do with it?

- What fictional character do you relate to most?

- If you could teleport us to anywhere in the world right now, where would it be?

- When did you feel the biggest adrenaline rush?

- What's an embarrassing story you have that most people don't know?

- What's your guilty pleasure?

- What's your most prized possession and why?

- If you could have a superpower, which would you choose?

- What does a perfect day look like to you?

WAYS TO FALL EVEN MORE IN LOVE WITH YOUR PARTNER

||||||||||

"Awake my sleeping bones; shake my settled soul. Show me the world through your eyes, because I crave something new."

Falling in love is one of the best relationship milestones. But I've always wondered if it's something that can only happen once? For a relationship that could possibly last a lifetime, I don't buy into the notion that falling in love is a one-time occurrence. The phrase is "falling in love" and not "fell into love" after all. That verb is ongoing. And in today's society, being intentional about falling in love over and over is needed.

The truth of modern times is that we're all crazy busy and distracted. If it's not your work or family or the dog needing to go for a walk, it's the phone that's essentially glued to your hands. Responsibilities fill up our schedule and waking thoughts.

When it comes to your relationship, you can't let these obstacles get in the way of fostering the love between you two. I'll be the first person to say I've been guilty of this: I compare my relationship to strangers I see on social media and take out the stress from my work on my boyfriend. But if I'm not aware of these actions, they can easily ruin this amazing relationship I have going for me.

If you think about it, there's no measure for love, just like there's no measure for any feeling; every emotion is relative. Your love for your partner will ebb and flow throughout your relationship. I know mine does. Some days Nish will do everything wrong; forget to take out the trash and use a tone that hurts my feelings. He'll get under my skin and I'll need my space from him. But the next day (or even mere hours later), I'll be hugging and kissing him. My boyfriend will be back to being one of my favorite people in this world.

So while life can distract us from what matters and love can fluctuate throughout a relationship, I've found there are ways to strengthen that love and build upon it. It's intentional actions that create more of the idea of "falling in love" with your partner; the sharing and acceptance of your feelings. You form a deeper bond with a person when your emotions are out on the table, and you witness them being accepted and understood.

If you're looking to fall even more in love with your partner, try these feeling-focused ways:

LET YOUR PARTNER KNOW YOUR GREATEST FEARS

We all worry about something in life. Maybe you fear the day your parents pass away or worry you'll never amount to anything. I have a tiny pit in my stomach that feels anxiety around where my life is heading and that at any point, the people I love most will abandon me. Whatever your fear is, it's a heavy burden to carry.

Sit your partner down one day (when you have free time and a heads-up about this serious talk) and explain what your greatest fears are in life. Talk about how they affect you and why you think your fears were created. Let your partner know you're not sharing these feelings with the hopes they can fix them—rather, you just want to be understood. Then allow your partner space to do the same with their fears.

SHARE PARTS OF YOUR PAST YOU DON'T SHARE WITH OTHERS

I had a hard time sharing my history of depression with Nish. I felt ashamed. I felt unlovable. But my past is not something to be ashamed of; everyone has been through something. What matters is who I am today. Sharing the not-so-stellar parts of your past takes away the secrecy you've held onto throughout your life. You're putting your cards on the table and giving your partner a chance to love you regardless.

And when they do, which they most likely will (unless they're an asshat), you're going to feel a kind of love you never thought you would. There's nothing quite like being completely honest about the events that shaped you into who you are today, especially the parts of your past you don't like.

SHOW YOUR PARTNER APPRECIATION EVERY DAY

Relationships are bound to hit a plateau. When you see someone all the time, you start to become used to their presence. It becomes your new normal. If you're not careful, though, you can start to take your partner for granted. The days of wonder and excitement when you're going on your first date or saying "I love you" for the first time might be over, but that doesn't mean you should stop showing them your appreciation.

Everyone shows their affection for people in different ways. Maybe you prefer giving your partner a back rub or taking out the garbage or surprising them with their favorite slice of cake (vanilla, please!). Keep showing your appreciation for them. Don't let that flame burn out.

TALK ABOUT YOUR LOVE LANGUAGES

If you aren't familiar with love languages, you want to be. I talk about them constantly in my writing, and they've helped me not only be a better girlfriend but ask for love in the ways I need it. I'll give you a little overview, but the creator of the theory, Gary Chapman, wrote a fantastic book on the subject called *The Five Love Languages*.

If you've ever thought that people show and receive love in different ways, you're correct. There are five love languages that most people have: words of affirmation, quality time, acts of service, physical touch, and gift-giving. I'm a words of affirmation kind of woman; I prefer hearing my boyfriend loves me more than going on a fancy dinner together. For him, he receives love best in the form of physical touch; he's the king of cuddling.

If you don't already know your love language, think about which ones feel most like the ways you receive and give love (they might be different). Then tell your partner you want to do a relationship activity; sit them down, explain what love languages are, and talk about what yours is while helping them figure out their love language. Knowing this information will help you both show love to each other in a way that you receive it best.

SPEND A WEEKEND ALONE, TOGETHER

Let me be clear: a weekend alone together that isn't in your apartment.

When you're always at each other's place, you're going to become comfortable in those environments. That's fine and totally normal. But why not shake things up?

Go for a weekend trip somewhere. Do whatever activities you both enjoy. When you're having fun and doing things out of the ordinary, you're your happiest selves—a state that most people don't experience often, especially if work and life get in the way. Seeing your partner in this state will also remind you of the parts of them you don't see often; the parts you most likely fell in love with in the first place.

PUT DOWN YOUR PHONE AND SIMPLY BE WITH THEM

When you sit down for a dinner night out, do you reach for your phone while you wait for the server, or do you have a conversation with your partner? Your answer to that question is very telling of how present you are during your time with your partner.

The more comfortable a couple gets in a relationship, the more they tend to take their time together for granted. My boyfriend and I will be on our phones for half of a dinner unless we're intentional about it. Sometimes, it's not a big deal. After all, we live together. Some dinners are quick, and we don't mind shutting off and mindlessly scrolling through social media.

But other nights, we set aside our phones and have deep conversations; something that a lot of people struggle with in their own homes. Without a doubt, every time we're out to dinner, we put our phones away and are present.

If you struggle with this same phone addiction, opt to leave your phone in your purse, pocket, or at home while you're on a date with your partner. I promise, when your presence isn't being interrupted with every ding from your phone, you'll have more in-depth conversations and meaningful interactions.

LEARN HOW TO COMMUNICATE DURING DISAGREEMENTS

How can you fall deeper in love with someone who is petty, yells, and gets mean with you any time you argue? Hint: you can't.

Instead, learn how to communicate your feelings better (refer to the chapter, "The Do's and Don'ts of Arguing"). Remember that you and your partner are a team. It's not about who is right; it's about coming to a mutual understanding.

By becoming better at arguing, you and your partner will feel safer and more understood in the relationship, and the terrible fights will diminish.

TELL YOUR PARTNER WHY YOU'RE ATTRACTED TO THEM

No one is a mind reader. Your partner can't magically know what you love about them. When my boyfriend is strumming on his guitar or smiles at me in a way that makes my heart melt, I tell him.

Whenever your partner does something you love, don't hesitate to blurt it out to them right then and there. Telling them about the things you love will end up making them want to do those things more (bonus points). At the same time, you don't need a reason to tell them why you love them. Chances are, you have a list of reasons. Randomly tell your partner things like how you knew you first loved them. Describe the special or unique qualities they have that make you feel crazy about them.

Hearing specifically why your partner loves you is like falling in love all over. If you haven't tried it, I suggest you do so ASAP.

If you're willing to be open with your feelings, falling in love is something that can happen multiple times with your partner. I'd even argue it's something we should all aim for.

Because everyone can use a little more love.

LASTING LOVE COMES DOWN TO ONE CHOICE

||||||||||

"Love is the ashes you're left with once passion has burned away. It's what exists on the days they drive you crazy, but the next day they're your favorite person. Love isn't a feeling because those come and go; it wouldn't last if that were the case. Love is what's uncovered when all the pretty bits have fallen away, and you still choose to love one another."

Back when I was dating Brad, my best friend's roommate at the time, he came to me with excitement one day, "let's do these 36 questions posted by the *New York Times*! They're supposed to create deep intimacy between two people." Being a highly emotional person, I was in.

The researchers who designed the questions claimed they would make two people fall in love with a simple list. The questions started light and simple but slowly became more profound. So, Brad and I went through each one, in order. And, though the questions helped us understand each other on a deeper level and even shed some tears, we did not fall in love.

This perplexed me. When we broke up, I thought back to those questions. It felt like he peered into my soul, took a look around, and decided it wasn't for him. Leaving me behind thinking, "Wait... I don't share that stuff with just *anyone!*"

But Brad and I dated almost three years ago. And though we didn't fall in love, I did with many men before him. Five, to be exact. Five men that, at their respective times, claimed to love me until the end. So why, then, am I just with one man? Why is it that the guy I call my boyfriend prevailed over the others?

Well, obviously, each failed relationship had its own unique defects.

So, a better question is, why can I believe the love that my boyfriend gives me this time?

Loving is a unique ability only humans can create awareness around. It's an art because we can improve upon the skill, sort of like a craft. As the author of *The Five Love Languages*, Gary Chapman, stated, "Falling in love is easy. Staying in love—that's the challenge."

> **BUT TO EVEN CONSIDER STAYING IN LOVE, WE HAVE TO MAKE A CHOICE: AT THE LOW POINTS, IN THE TIME OF DOUBT, WILL WE KEEP CHOOSING LOVE? AND ARE WE WILLING TO DO SO EVEN IF THE PERSON MAY NOT CHOOSE US ONE DAY?**

The uncertainties in love are scary. How can we know someone will make a great partner? Father? Bingo teammate well into retirement? How can we know we won't be betrayed? Our hearts not crushed? Our love not taken advantage of?

And the answer is plain and simple: *we don't.* We don't know how our lives will play out, and that runs true, especially when it comes to love. But just because we can't be certain, doesn't mean we can't try.

Loving is a choice. You find a person who makes your heart flutter and whose company you thoroughly enjoy; you understand each other, you could see yourself growing old with them.

So, you choose them; you choose a life with them. But it won't be the only time you'll have to choose them.

Because the doubt will creep in. They'll eventually hurt or disappoint you. And the choice to keep loving them comes down to your capabilities and willingness of working through the inevitable low points because being with them surpasses everything else.

I hear my current boyfriend's words trickle out of his mouth, "I love you, and I want to be with you forever." But how do I know his words of forever are true? I don't. But I can trust (because of the work I mentioned in the earlier chapter) that he's choosing me, and that's the biggest part of this equation. He chooses me. I choose him. That equals, I hope, lasting love.

We have open and honest communication, regularly checking in on one another. We both have space to speak our emotions, fears, and appreciations. We acknowledge the hard times will come, but we're certain we have what it takes to get through them. And all of this wrapped up into a package labeled "our love" seems like it will withstand time more than passion and lust ever would. But all because we are both making a choice.

I once listened to a talk online by a woman that did a questionnaire with a man that led them to fall in love. That woman, Mandy Len Catron, wrote the initial article that made famous those 36 questions Brad and I asked each other.

Readers wanted to understand the magic of Catron's relationship's success; everyone wanted to know if she and the man she did the questions with were still together. But Catron was wary of answering because the success of their relationship wasn't based on 36 questions designed for creating love. The success of their relationship hung on one main thing: a choice.

The two chose to love each other. Just like Brad and I chose not to. Just like Sean and I chose to stop. Just like all my exes chose not to. And just like my current boyfriend and I choose to.

Sure, love is a bit more nuanced and complex. But lasting love—that kind you see people having that spans a lifetime—is not.

You'll never find a perfect person who won't disappoint. Every single relationship is going to have its lows. And when those lows come, you'll have to make a choice.

In the end, that's the secret to lasting love.

KIRSTIE TAYLOR is a dating and relationship writer who found a loyal internet following through her candid essays. Her work has been featured in *Cosmopolitan Magazine, Well + Good,* and *The Washington Post's, The Lily.* She currently lives in Los Angeles, where she continues to write words that help people with their biggest struggles in love.

INSTAGRAM.COM/WORDSWITHKIRSTIE
KIRSTIETAYLOR.SUBSTACK.COM
KIRSTIETAYLOR.COM
TIKTOK.COM/@KIRSTIETAYLORR